THE HAT BOOK

THE HAT BOOK

CREATING HATS FOR EVERY OCCASION

JULIET BAWDEN

Dedication
For Douglas Bullock because he looks
sensational in a hat.

First published 1992
by Charles Letts & Co Ltd
Letts of London House
Parkgate Road
London SW11 4NQ

Designed and edited by
Anness Publishing Ltd
Boundary Row Studios
1 Boundary Row
London SE1 8HP

ISBN 1-85238-332-1

A CIP catalogue record for this book is available
from the British Library.

'Letts' is a registered trademark of
Charles Letts & Co Ltd

Editorial Director: Joanna Lorenz
Project Editor: Judith Simons
Designer: Kit Johnson
Photographers: Jan Baldwin and Brian Leonard
Stylist: Cathy Sinker
Illustrator: Tim Pearce

Credits
The author and publishers would like to thank the
following for additional photographs: Bailey and
Tomlin, page 15 *t*; Graham Smith/Kangol, page 15
br; Oxfam, page 12 *tl* (Peter McCulloch), 12 *tr*
(Caroline Lucas), 12 *b* (M Pocock); Philip Treacy,
page 14; Visual Arts Library, page 10 *t c b*.

Printed in Hong Kong

Contents

Introduction

Not so long ago, a hat was seen not only as something that protected you from the rain and cold, but as a stylish and highly versatile accessory that could offset and flatter an outfit, frame a face in a becoming way, and as a feature that could express the wearer's mood or even alter it. Yet in more recent years, it seemed as if the majority of people were hard pressed to produce a suitable model for even a wedding or funeral. The 1960s and 1970s saw an end to formal dressing, and there was less and less demand for 'dress' hats; as a result many milliners went out of business.

This relative neglect of the hat over recent history can perhaps be interpreted as an act of social rebellion, as part of the general rejection of traditional dress expectations. The international fashion journalist Brenda Polen stated as much in a recent article: 'Hats tend to be one of the safest, most easily read symbols that the lexicon of human apparel offers us. One of the great post-war acts of rebellion, in keeping with an egalitarian refusal to be categorized at first sight, was the popular renunciation of the hat. And if it were not so, that rarity, the truly opinionated hat, would be powerless as a tool of subversion. And powerless it certainly is not.' (*Departures*, June/July 1991)

Now, however, the hat is resuming its rightful place in our fashion vocabulary. According to market research, there was a growth rate in the wearing of hats in the United Kingdom of one-third between 1984 and 1989, with a 13 per cent rise between 1988 and 1989. In the United States there was a comparable rise in the popularity of the hat, with a profit leap of $300 million to $350 million between 1986 and 1987. This leap is believed by those in the trade to have been initiated by the 1986/7 Paris collection, which brought in more structured clothes that required sophisticated accessories such as hats. It has been suggested by more than one person in the hat business, including Bill Horseman, Chairman of the Millinery Guild in Great Britain, that the revival of hats as a main fashion item is also due to the Princess of Wales, 'The patron saint of modern millinery'. This revived interest in hat wearing generally has led in turn to more fashion students specializing in hat design and setting up on their own as independent milliners.

Wearing a hat, other than as part of a uniform, certainly gets you noticed. The international milliner Graham Smith tells a story of persuading his mother to wear an outrageous creation to a party: 'She burst into tears in the taxi. She felt absolutely ghastly when she walked in – but it was such a conversation piece that she was immediately whisked away and I didn't see her again all evening. A good hat can be wonderful morale.' Shirley Hex, who

started making hats at 15 and taught millinery at the Royal College of Art in London to many now-famous hat makers, says: 'If I don't wear a hat, things don't happen to me. So I wear one every day — people give me seats on buses and stop their cars at zebra crossings.'

This volume introduces you to some of the most exciting contemporary designs in hat fashion today, and draws on the ideas of the best young hatters to provide all the practical techniques, ideas and confidence necessary to create and adapt your own wonderful hats at home. In the following pages you will find hats and hat accessories suitable for every occasion, for every season, for every style, and for men, women and children. *The Hat Book* will, it is hoped, inspire you to add style and excitement to your wardrobe with your own exuberant collection of creative, home-made designer hats!

A feminine and elegant hat, this large straw is decorated with a flamboyant bow in fuchsia pink. Worn with confidence and the right clothes, the effect is stunning. (*Above*)

Historical overview

For centuries hats have been a sartorial status symbol, displaying wealth, nationality, status, political beliefs, religion and occupation. In the Roman Empire, to be crowned with a laurel wreath was a mark of great honour. Aristocratic ladies wore jewelled head-dresses to show their standing in the community. In ancient Greece and Rome a hat was the right of free citizens but not of slaves. In Renaissance Italy each leading family had its own distinctive style of hat with its own colour and design as a visible reminder of its power, patronage and politics. In coronation ceremonies the exchange of a crown marks stages in regal authority.

The Church in the Middle Ages required married women to cover their hair in public with hoods or veils. During the fourteenth century women began to wear hats of the current masculine style for riding and travelling, and by the reign of Elizabeth I (1558–1603) hats were worn for other occasions.

Fashion hats

At the beginning of the seventeenth century the fashion was for a hat known as the 'coptain'. It was tall with a slightly tapered crown and a moderate brim. This style is believed to have originated in Spain in the middle of the sixteenth century. During the reign of James I (1603–1625) these hats were made from a variety of materials including felt, beaver and stiffened silk and velvet. They were usually black although occasionally they would be coloured. Often they were adorned with jewelled brooches or hatbands. The coptain tended to be worn by men at an angle and by women perched straight on their heads. With Charles I (1625–1649) came the well-known Cavalier hat, with its wider, usually more flexible brim and lower crown. This hat was worn by both men and women. English Puritan women continued to wear the coptain over white bonnets.

After 1630 the style of men's and women's hats became increasingly different from each other. At this time upper-class women in particular were wearing their hair in a pretty, loose corkscrew-curled fashion which they were reluctant to cover. This led to different fashions for different seasons. In spring the head might be completely uncovered, while in summer a light veil might be worn, and in winter a dark silk hood gathered loosely at the neck might be chosen.

The history of hats has always been entwined with the history of hairstyles and this was particularly so after the Restoration (1660) when hairstyles became increasingly elaborate with many curls which were wired to stand out from the head. This led to a decline in hat wearing.

Night caps

Caps were worn by men informally indoors from the sixteenth century to the end of the nineteenth century. Although they were not for wearing to bed they were known as night caps. The style changed very little over the centuries. It had a deep round crown made from four conical segments with the border turned up to form a close brim. It was usually made from silk, wool or velvet. The seventeenth-century caps were sometimes quilted and embroidered. After 1730 the night cap took on a more Eastern look and became more turban-like in appearance. In the 1850s the design underwent another transformation and the cap evolved into the style of the smoking cap, a style which has become popular again today with both sexes.

While men wore night caps, women wore small round caps often trimmed with great quantities of lace and ribbon. As hairstyles changed so did the styles and sizes of the caps. During the 1770s and 1780s hairstyles grew to a fantastic size and caps for undress wear were similarly large in scale, while dress caps were tiny. During the 1790s caps for day wear became less fashionable but it was not until the 1870s that caps ceased to be worn by women other than at breakfast. Eventually, the style died out altogether by the start of World War I.

For outdoor wear, flat caps were worn by sixteenth-century artisans and tradespeople, and cloth-caps by working people in the 1920s and 1930s.

Straw hats

In the 1730s the fashion for rustic straw hats appeared and later in the eighteenth century the shepherdess or milkmaid dress was created to go with it, to be worn to masked balls and pageants.

The earliest record of English straw plaiting is 1681 when a Thomas Baskerville noted that some of the people of Dunstable, Bedfordshire, were making straw hats. Only seven years later a petition was to show that 14,000 people in the counties of Bedfordshire, Buckinghamshire and Hertfordshire made their living from making straw hats. The shepherdess hat from this period was fashionable from the 1730s to the 1770s.

In France during the 1760s the professions of hairdressing and millinery emerged and both were to have a profound effect upon women's hats. The rustic English straw hat was taken up by the French and given a touch of French chic. This included a profusion of new trimmings including artificial flowers and interesting new shapes. It is from this time that millinery, as we know it today, really took off. For outdoor wear, straw hats were popular, especially in the form of poke-bonnets.

Modern influences

In the nineteenth century, the rise of the middle classes and the growth in leisure time gave more people money to spend on luxury items such as hats. Newspapers and ladies' magazines gave guidance as to what was the latest in millinery fashion and magazines also published patterns for caps. Throughout the twentieth century styles in hats have changed to suit the fashion in dress styles. The Twenties are as well known for the neat head-hugging cloche hat as for the straight up-and-down dresses of the flapper girls.

Hollywood was to have a great influence on the style of hats throughout the Thirties and Forties and even at the decline of the hat industry in the 1960s it was the film *Bonnie and Clyde* which persuaded women to start wearing berets once more. The Seventies too were lean years for milliners. Films such as *The Great Gatsby* revived the Twenties look and beaded caps became the rage for parties. The film *Annie Hall* brought with it the fashion for women wearing large men's hats pulled down low over their forehead. It became apparent that a man's hat made a woman look frail and sexy.

Hats today

The 1980s saw a great revival in hats as worn by pop stars and other media personalities. People wanting much more freedom of expression in how they chose to dress started wearing hats again. In consequence, many new milliners started businesses and specialist shops further encouraged the trend in hat wearing – a trend that is happily still continuing.

*A*n apprentice carpet weaver wears a typical Afghan hat. The shape is similar to that of a smoking cap and it is entirely decorated with cross-stitch embroidery. (*Above*)

Folk traditions

*T*his Mien child from Northern Thailand wears a distinctive hat decorated with large red pom-poms, beads and decorative embroidery. *(Opposite, top)*

*T*urbans, worn as a protection against the fierce sun, are traditional to many hot countries. These brightly coloured turbans are worn by women in Guatemala, South America. *(Opposite, bottom)*

The term folk costume usually suggests costumes of the past. For although most countries have a traditional peasant costume by which they may be regionally or nationally identified, in the twentieth century people all over the world tend to dress in a similar manner. This is due to a number of factors, such as cheap and easy methods of manufacture and the growth of the communication, advertising and fashion industries.

Costumes of the past, and in some cases the present, were often designed with very practical aspects in mind. These would include the materials available, climate and often ideas of propriety. Hats have always been an important part of folk costume; they keep the sun off the head in hot weather, they keep in warmth in winter and, in some countries, provide a modest cover for women.

In countries with a hot climate, people tend to wear hats with large brims which cover the face and head. Or they wear turbans which, depending on the part of the world from which they come, may be very large or small and tight. In Afghanistan turbans are tied under the chin or with a tail which trails over the shoulder and acts as a dust veil or pocket handkerchief. Liberian women wear turbans of striped cloth while Nigerians wear turbans which have been dyed in indigo. In countries such as Algeria, Arabia and Morocco people wear flowing robes which cover the head and the entire body.

Countries which do not share a common history but do share a common industry often have similar shaped hats or hats with similar forms of decoration. For example, France, Finland, Estonia, Austria, Czechoslovakia and Switzerland all have in common highly developed lace and embroidery skills which are shown to good effect in their women's hats.

Variations on a theme

Hats which have their foundations in folk tradition are often picked up by the fashion industry and subtly altered to suit the mood of the time. The beret so popular today has its roots in the Scottish Highland 'blue bonnet'. A similar kind of tam-o'-shanter style is worn in some parts of Greece. The bowler which has been popularized by Fred Bare in the United Kingdom with its distinctive style of embroidery, has its origins in Peruvian women's hats.

The ever-popular smoking-style cap appears in many national costumes from Macedonia, Pakistan and Malaysia. Sometimes it is the colour or pattern of folk hats which inspires new designs, or sometimes it is the shape or the material used. Museums of costume have many examples of hats which can provide inspiration.

International style

Once upon a time, women craved a French label in a hat; now the covetable labels are British: Graham Smith, Australian-born Frederick Fox, Stephen Jones, Irish-born Philip Treacy, Philip Somerville, and John Boyd, to name a few. The Royal College of Art in London has at last created a post-graduate place for a fashion student to study millinery – and its very first graduate was Treacy, recently the star of the 1992 Karl Lagerfeld/Chanel Paris show with his startling range of hat creations. Treacy's unprecedented rise to fame in just one year since leaving college shows the new and important role milliners are now playing in the fashion business.

Many of these hat makers are now better known to the general public than fashion designers. The most well-known hat maker is probably David Shilling, who has been promoting millinery as an applied art for many years, creating show hats for Ascot and other high-profile events as well as contributing to and organizing exhibitions of his hats in museums. But each country has its own galaxy of talent. As the world gets increasingly easy to travel, hat makers are jet-setting from one continent to the next working with different fashion designers. While most designers like to make hats for their own private customers, many also design diffusion or cheaper ranges of hats for retail outlets, or they work on specific collections with dress designers. For example, Viv Knowland produces her own hats, but also works as a design consultant for Laura Ashley, Next and Jaeger; and Treacy is now designing for Marc Bohan, Norman Hartnell, Rifat Ozbek and John Galliano.

One of the most exciting innovations in hat design is the appearance of milliners who originally trained in other disciplines, be it textile design, ceramics, felt-making, jewellery, graphics, or weaving and knitting. Bridget Bailey and Anne Tomlin, who are behind the label Bailey and Tomlin, originally trained in woven textile design, for instance. Their soft and romantic hats incorporate strong textural details, such as printed, pleated and moulded forms which have international appeal. This new breed of milliner heralds a truly eclectic approach to hat design.

Clockwise from top: examples of stylish hats from three influential designers – Bailey and Tomlin, Graham Smith and Viv Knowland.

Design considerations

It is essential to choose a well-fitting hat, which feels comfortable to wear and which suits your colouring and clothing. This soft and flattering felt tricorn hat is decorated with twirls of frogging and an ostrich plume. It could be worn with any fashionable winter outfit. (Right: Herald and Heart Hatters)

We no longer have to wear hats only in extreme weather conditions; moreover, dress codes are less formal and styles freer than in the first six decades of this century. Therefore, anyone wearing a hat today is making a fashion statement, aware that this important accessory denotes a sense of presence and style. A well-chosen hat should complement, not overshadow, the wearer and it should be a natural part of the outfit you are wearing.

There are, therefore, many aspects to consider before buying or making a hat of your own. Does the colour or style flatter you? Is it suitable for the occasion? Will it dominate or blend in with the outfit? Also, choose a hat that will blend with your skin tone. If the basic colour and shape are right, then consider the trimming. Remember, it can be easily changed to match some part of the outfit (see Embellishing Hats, pages 100–121).

In the same way that only certain hairstyles will flatter, not all hats will look good, so here are some ideas to help you choose the right hat. Go into a hat shop or department store and try on hats in a whole range of different styles to get the feel of which shapes are most suitable. Rearrange your hair to see what effect this has on the general look. Always use a full-length mirror when trying on hats – the hat should balance the waistline, neckline and hem. It should fit perfectly and feel comfortable on the head. Too small and it will feel unbalanced; too large and you may have difficulty seeing where you are going. Remember if you are planning to add embellishments that they can alter the proportions considerably, especially if they are dramatic trimmings such as large fabric flowers or sweeping feathers.

Face shapes

Here are a few guidelines to help you match different shapes of face to styles of hat. They are just guidelines and there are a few tricks to get round them. For example, if you are big and want to wear a small hat, choose one with veiling or decorations which add width.

SQUARE FACE

Wear the hat at a slant or tilt or have the brim asymmetrical.

NARROW FACE

Avoid tall narrow hats. Experiment with brims and full hats.

WIDE FACE

Off-the-face styles, Bretons or pillboxes on the back of the head are all suitable.

ROUND FACE

Do not choose fez or flowerpot-shaped hats. Big hats are good, as are hats with brims, but only when worn at an angle. The crown should never be narrower than the face unless the brim is the most prominent feature.

HEART-SHAPED FACE

People who have wide cheekbones or a heart-shaped face will look good in almost any style hat – head-hugging turbans, cloches, picture hats, sailor hats or boaters. Wear them straight across the brow and straight across the hairline. Make sure that the crown is never narrower than the width of the cheekbones.

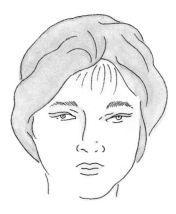

BIG NOSE

Wear a hat so that it sits forward on the face rather than at the back of the head. Brims and peaks can be worn, with the object of drawing attention to the peak or brim and not the nose.

Hat styles

Hat fashions change all the time with crowns getting taller or more squat, and brims increasing and diminishing in size. When looking at old family photos it is often a hat which will indicate most clearly in which decade the photo was taken. Here are some of the main styles.

BERET

Berets come in all sizes. The small Basque beret emanated from France during World War I. The tam-o'-shanter is a larger, Scottish version of the beret.

PILLBOX

This hat has a round, flat top and is worn high on the head, often at a slight angle.

CLOCHE

Cloche is the French word for bell. The hat turns down all round and often frames the face.

TOQUE

A small decorative hat not unlike a beret in shape, it is sometimes covered with folds of material, such as organza or silk.

TURBAN

A milliner's form of the Eastern head-dress, the turban consists of material draped gracefully round the head, following the shape of the skull at the back, with a raised knot or folds in the front. It is a soft and flattering style for older women.

BRETON

This hat reproduces the shape of straw hats worn by Breton sailors. The brim turns up all the way round.

CAP

A small, tight-fitting hat, it clings closely to the head. It is sometimes called a Juliet cap or skull-cap.

CARTWHEEL

This has a large, flat, circular brim and is one of the most dramatic forms of hat.

PICTURE HAT

The brim of this hat is large and it dips at the back and the front. A very decorative style associated with Royal Ascot, garden parties or wedding hats, this hat is best made of fine straw with decorations in chiffon and lace.

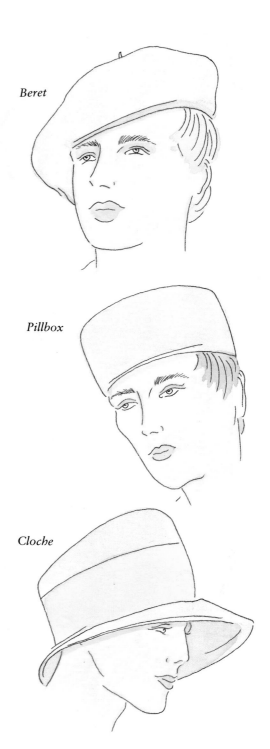

Beret

Pillbox

Cloche

Toque

Cap

Turban

Cartwheel

Breton

Picture hat

MEN'S HATS

The Panama hat, trilby, flat cap, bowler, boater, top hat and flying helmet are perennial styles of men's hats. They have been borrowed for women's hats, too, over the years.

CREATING HATS

Many artists who originally trained in other disciplines – textile design, ceramics, felt-making, jewellery, graphics, weaving and knitting – are directing their talents towards hats and are discovering them to be a versatile medium in which to express their creativity. Some of their wonderful designs are featured in the following pages, which offer step-by-step guidance to making and rejuvenating a wide range of hats, from traditional straws and felts to fun hats for everyday wear. Most of the hats only require basic sewing skills, materials and equipment, but refer to the Practicalities section for special techniques and sewing stitches. Follow the instructions and photographs and you will find that creating beautiful and exciting hats is fun, affordable and achievable.

Smart straw

Transform a plain straw hat into an archetypal summer hat for 'the season': a day at the races, a smart garden party or a wedding, perhaps. This unusual green straw with its contrasting black trim is very striking, but the colours and embellishment may be adapted to suit any summer straw hat. For example, try other classic colour combinations such as navy and white, or fuchsia pink and purple; black and white is a particularly classy teaming. Vary the trim, too, using ribbon bows, feathers, or a more exaggerated swathe of veiling. The variations are endless.

PREPARATION

Sew in the top edge of the headband to the head fitting by hand.

MATERIALS & EQUIPMENT

2 cm (¾ in) wide petersham ribbon for headband (circumference of head plus 2 cm/¾ in overlap)

basic straw hat

thread

millinery wire (circumference of brim)

1 cm (⅜ in) wide petersham ribbon (circumference of brim plus 2 cm/¾ in overlap)

2 cm (¾ in) wide petersham ribbon (circumference of crown plus overlap)

net

roses and leaves trim to match ribbons and net

needle
sewing machine
dressmaking scissors
iron

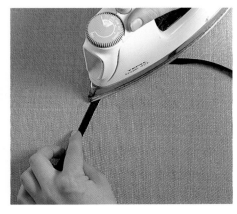

1   Wire the edge of the brim using a machine set to a large widely spaced zigzag stitch.

2   Cut enough 1 cm (⅜ in) petersham ribbon to go round the edge of the brim with a 2 cm (¾ in) overlap. Fold the ribbon in half lengthways, curve it round and iron, curving and stretching as you go.

This hat is smart enough to wear to any occasion. The brim is wired, and edged with black petersham to match the hatband, the two flower trims and the net on top of the crown.
(*Opposite*)

This large black straw picture hat also offers a strong contrast in colour. Decorated with pink feathers, black grosgrain and pink moiré bows, the trimmings are lavish but easy to make. (*Right: Herald and Heart Hatters*)

3 Using a medium straight stitch, machine the petersham band on to the brim edge starting and finishing at the back. Ease it while stitching to ensure a snug fit. If unsure of this step, the ribbon can be sewn on by hand using small stab stitches.

4 Sew the wider petersham ribbon on to the crown. Match up the join at the back so that it is in line with the join of the band edge on the brim.

5 Pin the net on to and over the crown, then stitch. The secret is to catch the net at only four or five points around the crown and not to anchor it totally into position.

6 Sew on the roses and leaves trim. Rather than positioning one rose at the back of the hat, try something a little more unusual and sew trims on either side of the crown, as here.

Smoking cap

This style of hat was popular in the 1860s and 1870s and was known as a man's smoking cap. It was often highly embellished with silk braid, tassels, appliqué or intricate patchwork designs. The crown and the band may be decorated, or one or the other can be left plain. You do not need special millinery tools or techniques to make this style of hat, just a domestic sewing machine and a great deal of care!

The hat featured was made from silk dupion, which is a heavyweight raw silk similar to slub silk, but you may use any fabric ranging from cotton, corduroy, velvet, brocade to fine fabrics.

PREPARATION

Either trace or photocopy the segment pattern six times and enlarge to the dimensions detailed on the pattern.

The segment has been reproduced at half its actual size. Cut out six paper segment pieces.

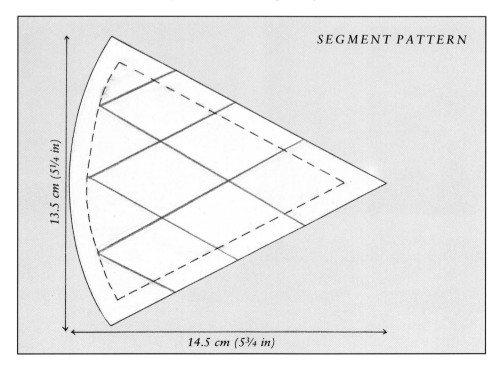

SEGMENT PATTERN

13.5 cm (5¼ in)

14.5 cm (5¾ in)

MATERIALS & EQUIPMENT

30 × 40 cm (12 × 16 in) black silk dupion

50 × 100 cm (20 × 40 in) iron-on webbing

50 × 100 cm (20 × 40 in) gold silk dupion

50 × 100 cm (20 × 40 in) thin polyester wadding

10 cm × 75 cm (4 × 30 in) Vilene or other stiff interfacing

50 × 100 cm (20 × 40 in) butter muslin (cheesecloth)

black and red thread

10 × 10 cm (4 × 4 in) red silk dupion

button kit for covered button

120 cm (47 in) thin piping cord

50 × 100 cm (20 × 40 in) acetate lining

tracing paper
ruler
pencil
paper scissors
dressmakers' pins
iron
dressmaking scissors
sewing machine
tiny coin or washer
needle

This appliqué hat suits most people, male or female.
(Opposite: Sarah King)

A 1 cm (³/₈ in) seam allowance is included in the pattern. Cut a paper pattern for the hatband 70 × 8 cm (27½ × 3¼ in). Pin the paper segments together to form a circle, then pin these to the hatband and try the paper hat on. Adjust to fit. Iron the black silk to the iron-on webbing. Draw the diamond design on the paper, and then cut out.

Cut a 70 × 8 cm (27½ × 3¼ in) piece in each of the gold silk dupion, wadding and Vilene or interfacing (or to altered hatband measurement). Sandwich together with wadding in the middle. Make a second sandwich replacing the Vilene with butter muslin, cut to 30 × 40 cm (12 × 16 in) and, using the fabric segment as a guide, baste the three layers together.

1 Following the webbing manufacturer's instructions (for the temperature), iron the black diamonds on to the fabric and wadding sandwich. Set the machine to a very close, small zigzag stitch and appliqué the black fabric to the gold.

2 Cut out each segment and then machine together down each straight edge, until the crown of the hat is complete.

3 Iron the red silk on to the iron-on webbing. Use a tiny coin or washer to draw round and then cut out lots of red dots. Using red thread, appliqué the dots into position. Cover the button with red silk and sew this to the apex of the crown.

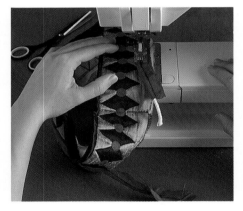

4 Cut the piping cord in half and then cut 2.5 cm (1 in) wide strips of red and black fabric on the bias. Use these strips to cover the piping cord. Edge the hatband with the fabric-covered piping cord.

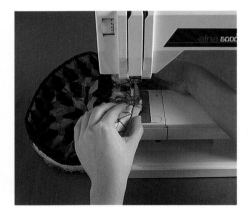

5 With right sides together, pin and then baste the hatband to the crown, try on and adjust to fit. Sew the two ends of the band together and then sew the crown on to the hatband.

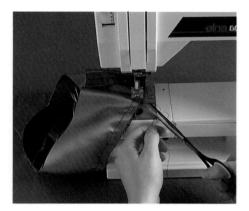

6 From lining fabric, cut a crown with a slightly larger circumference than that of the outside crown, and a lining band. With right sides facing, machine the band on to the crown.

7 With wrong sides together, pin the lining inside the hat. Sew the crown lining in place with stab stitches. Turn under the edge of the lining band and sew with a hemming stitch hiding all raw edges inside the hat.

These hats show how the smoking-cap pattern can be adapted. The light-coloured hats feature ribbon designs. The black and grey hat features the diamond pattern, finished off with a topknot. The final hat features multi-coloured kites.
(*Above: Sarah King*)

Cocktail hat

Cocktail hats are usually small and rather frivolous and tend to perch on the head. Jacquard weave and velvet were used here to cover the basic hat shape and to form the twisted trim, and a net bow provides the finishing touch. Cocktail hats can be made from any number of materials; but to begin with it is advisable to use heavier fabrics such as employed here, or try panne velvet, felts, heavyweight lace fabric or heavy silk satin. It is easy for glue to show through on lightweight materials, so until you are more experienced avoid light silks, jerseys and fine lace fabrics.

MATERIALS & EQUIPMENT

shape or straw crown cut from an old hat (ready-made net shapes are available from haberdashers in department stores)

circle of Jacquard weave fabric (to cover the hat plus at least 5 cm (2 in) allowance for turning)

thread

90 × 8 cm (36 × 3¼ in) velvet

90 × 8 cm (36 × 3¼ in) Jacquard weave

net

lining fabric (to cover inside of hat, plus seam allowance)

narrow elastic or a comb (to hold the hat in position)

fabric glue

needle

pins

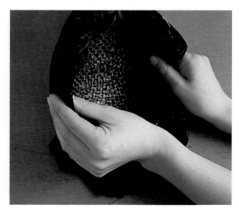

1 Holding the 'shape', cover up to 2 cm (¾ in) from the edge with glue all the way round.

2 Place the circle of fabric over the shape; pull evenly and ease out any folds. Fold the turning allowance under the rim of the shape.

The finished project hat is seen displayed on the stand. In the foreground is a variation, fit for a Christmas party, made of pink velvet and covered in holly leaves and trimmed with sequin-edged netting. (*Opposite*: variation: *Herald and Heart Hatters*)

3 Sew by hand, using tiny stitches to attach the fabric to the rim of the crown.

4 Make two fabric 'sausages' in contrast materials, one in the same Jacquard weave used to cover the hat and one in velvet, 8 cm (3¼ in) deep and 1¼ times the circumference of the crown.

5 Twist the sausages together and pin them on to the edge of the crown. Sew into place using invisible stitching. (See Decorating a Felt, pages 74–75, for detailed instructions on making sausages.)

6 Gather and arrange the net into a false bow and sew this on to the back of the hat.

7 Make a lining for the hat by cutting a circle of fabric to fit inside plus seam allowance. Glue it inside the centre of the hat, turn under the raw edges and sew in place. To hold the hat in position, either sew a comb to the inside back of the hat or attach a length of elastic.

*T*wo simple yet elegant cocktail hats are covered in heavy lace, which imparts texture and subtle decoration. (*Right: Gilly Forge*)

Knitted tweed hat

This versatile hat, featuring a cable design and embroidery detail, can be made with or without earflaps. It is also very quick to knit; the measurements are for an average size head.

MATERIALS & EQUIPMENT

100 g (4 oz) Aran-weight (6-ply) tweed wool
contrast yarn for embroidery

pair 5 mm (No 6) needles
cable needle
4 double-ended 5 mm (No 6) needles
embroidery needle

Abbreviations

C8F = slip 4 sts on to cable needle and hold at front of work, knit 4, then knit 4 from cable needle; C8B = slip 4 sts on to cable needle and hold at back of work, knit 4, then knit 4 from cable needle. Skpo = slip 1, knit 1, pass slip stitch over.

Both hats are hand knitted and are shown in two different colourways; one features the optional earflaps. Note the contrasting embroidery detail in simple overstitch.
(*Left: Jennie Atkinson*)

Tension

17–18 stitches and 25–26 rows to 10 cm (4 in) square using stocking stitch and 5 mm (No 6) needles.

Band

Using 5 mm needles cast on 24 stitches.
Row 1 Knit 4, purl 2, knit 16, purl 2.
Row 2 Knit 2, purl 16, knit 6.
Row 3 As row 1.
Row 4 As row 2.
Row 5 Knit 4, purl 2, C8F twice, purl 2.
Row 6 As row 2.
Rows 7–10 Repeat rows 1 and 2 twice.
Row 11 Knit 4, purl 2, knit 4, C8B, knit 4, purl 2.
Row 12 As row 2.
Repeat rows 1–12 until work measures 50 cm (20 in) from beginning. Cast off.

Top

Using 5 mm (No 6) needles, cast on 96 stitches.
Round 1 Knit stitches on to four 5 mm (No 6) double-ended needles (32 stitches on each) and work in rounds. Knit 2 rounds.
Round 4 (Skpo, knit 12, knit 2 together) repeat 6 times. 84 sts. Knit 3 rounds.
Round 8 (Skpo, knit 10, knit 2 together) repeat 6 times. 72 sts. Knit 3 rounds.
Round 12 (Skpo, knit 8, knit 2 together) repeat 6 times. 60 sts. Continue to decrease in the same way on every 4th round until 24 rounds have been worked and 24 stitches remain. Break yarn and pull through remaining stitches and fasten down securely on inside.

Earflaps

(Make 2.) Using 5 mm (No 6) needles cast on 18 stitches.
Knit 28 rows in garter stitch.
Row 29 Knit 2 together, knit 14, knit 2 together.
Knit 2 rows.
Row 32 Knit 2 together, knit 12, knit 2 together.
Knit 2 rows.
Row 35 Knit 2 together, knit 10, knit 2 together.
Row 36 Knit.
Row 37 Knit 2 together, knit 8, knit 2 together.
Row 38 Knit 2 together, knit 6, knit 2 together.
Row 39 Knit 2 together, knit 4, knit 2 together.
Row 40 Knit 2 together, knit 2, knit 2 together.
Row 41 Knit 2 together twice.
Row 42 Knit 2 together. Break yarn and pull through remaining stitch, leaving an end of 15 cm (6 in).

To finish
Sew the band into a circle. Sew the top on to the band using a running stitch and with seam on the outside. Try on the hat and position the earflaps. Sew the earflaps to the inside of the hat 2.5 cm (1 in) from the bottom of the band.

Ties
(Make 2.) Take a piece of contrast yarn 100 cm (39 in) long. Fold in half and knot the ends together. Holding the knotted end securely in the left hand, insert the right forefinger in the fold of the yarn and twist yarn until it folds back on itself from the centre. Knot all the ends together. Use yarn ends left on the earflaps to sew the tie securely in place.

To embroider
Using contrast yarn, oversew around the seam between the band and the top. Stitch around the earflaps. Finally, stitch between the cable band and rib, catching the earflaps in place.

A large cable forms the hatbands of these knitted hats; a detail of the design is shown here. (*Above*)

Baby hat

Although called a baby hat, this simple knitted hat does in fact fit a child from 7 to 30 months depending on how much it is stretched. The one basic pattern can be used to make five very different hats.

MATERIALS & EQUIPMENT

50 g (4 oz) 4-ply wool in main colour for each hat

pair 3¼ mm (No 10) needles
To decorate: sequins, beads, fake metallic coins, diamanté and oddments of coloured wool for patterns

Tension
23 stitches and 33 rows to 10 cm (4 in) square using stocking stitch and 3¼ mm (No 10) needles.

Basic hat

Cast on 115 stitches.
Starting with a knit row, work in stocking stitch until hat measures 14 cm (5½ in) from the beginning, ending with a purl row.

To shape the top
Decrease row Knit 2, (knit 3 together, knit 3) 18 times, knit 3 together, knit 2. 77 stitches.
Work 3 rows straight.

Decrease row Knit 1, (knit 3 together, knit 1) 19 times. 39 stitches.
Decrease row Purl 1, (knit 2 together) to end. 20 stitches.
Break off the yarn, thread it through the remaining stitches and pull tight to fasten off.
Stitch the side seam of the hat.

Bobble hat

To make a Bobble:
Work (knit 1, purl 1) twice into next stitch. Turn and knit 4, turn and knit 4, turn and (knit 2 together) twice, turn and knit 2 together.

Following pattern for basic hat, work 10 rows in stocking stitch in black.

Next row Knit 2, (make bobble, knit 9) 11 times alternating red, yellow and green colours for bobbles, knit 3.
Work 9 rows straight.
Next row Knit 7, (make bobble, knit 9) 10 times, beginning with red then alternating the colours as before, knit 8.
Work 9 rows straight.

Next row Knit 2, (make bobble, knit 9) 11 times, beginning with green and alternating colours, knit 3.
Finish hat as for basic pattern from To Shape the Top.

To decorate
Make three bobbles, one in each colour, and sew to the top of the hat.

Pocket hat

Knit basic hat in stocking stitch, following the pattern.

Pocket
Cast on 15 stitches and, starting with a knit row, work in stocking stitch for 18 rows. Work 3 rows in garter stitch.
Cast off.
Sew pocket on to the hat.

Stalk
Cast on 40 stitches. Beginning with a knit row work 8 rows in stocking stitch. Cast off.
Roll the stalk lengthways and join at the seam.
Sew the end of the stalk to the top of the hat. Make a tassel and attach it to the other end.

To decorate
Decorate with fake metallic coins and sew tiny gold beads round the stalk.

Star hat

Knit basic hat in stocking stitch, following the pattern.

Stalk
Cast on 7 stitches and beginning with a knit row work 8 rows in stocking stitch. Cast off.

To make up
Roll the stalk lengthways and join the seam.
Stitch the side seam of the hat and attach the stalk at the top.

To decorate
Sew star sequins all over the hat. Anchor them into position with small pearl beads.

Strawberry hat

Following pattern for basic hat, work 4 cm (1½ in) stocking stitch in red wool, ending with a purl row.
Row 1 Knit (1 yellow, 3 red) to last 3 stitches, knit 1 yellow, 2 red.
Work 5 rows in red.
Row 7 Knit 2 red, 1 yellow, (3 red, 1 yellow) to end of row.
Work 5 rows in red.
Repeat rows 1–7 once.
Work 3 rows in red.

Leaves
Row 23 Knit 4 red, 1 green, (11 red, 1 green) to last 2 stitches, knit 2 red.

Row 24 Purl 1 red, (3 green, 9 red) to last 6 stitches, purl 3 green, 3 red. Continue increasing the number of green stitches and reducing the red stitches evenly until there are 11 green stitches to 1 red stitch ending with a purl row.
Working in green only, shape the top as for the basic pattern.

Stalk
Working in green make and finish as for Star Hat.

These little hats are soft, warm and light for a baby to wear. Shown here are the Star Hat (*opposite*) and the Strawberry Hat (*above*).

Snake hat

Following the basic hat pattern, work 10 rows in stocking stitch.
Make the snake following the chart given, either by knitting it in or by Swiss darning.
Finish as for the basic hat pattern. Decorate the snake's eyes and tongue with diamanté. Sew beads on to the green flecks in the pattern.

Note:
Some of these baby hats incorporate beads, sequins and fake gold coins as decoration. Ensure that these hats are only worn by a baby or young child under supervision as the small decorations could present a danger if chewed and swallowed.

*F*ive baby beanie hats made from the same basic pattern with various decorations. Clockwise from top: a soft green hat with a long tasselled stalk is decorated with gold beads and fake gold coins and a little white pocket; black hat with clusters of coloured bobbles; blue hat with sequin stars and a moon; navy hat with snake pattern decorated with diamanté; in the centre, strawberry design hat with a green stalk. (*Right:* made by *June Buckland*; decorated by *Jan Bridge*)

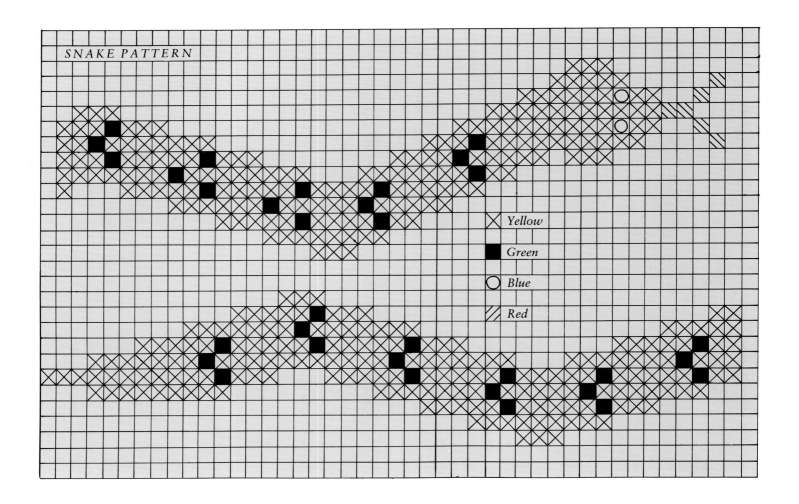

SNAKE PATTERN

✕ Yellow

■ Green

○ Blue

╱ Red

Castle hat

A soft, floppy dressmakers' hat, the castle hat is made from velvet and gets its name from the six 'crenellated' segments. This style suits both men and women and the size can be adjusted to fit either.

PREPARATION

The size given is for a head circumference of 60 cm (23½ in). To adjust the pattern to fit, measure the head circumference and divide the measurement by six. (There are six segments to the hat.) The bottom of each segment will be that measurement plus 1 cm (⅜ in) seam allowances.

Draw the pattern to the specified dimensions on dressmakers' grid paper. Cut out six pattern pieces for the main segments. Pin the main segments on to the velvet on the bias and cut out two each in purple, maroon and green.

The hatband may be cut on the straight grain of the fabric: cut a band 65.5 × 13.5 cm/25¾ × 5¼ in in black velvet, interfacing and lining fabric. From the lining fabric, cut a circle with an 18 cm (7 in) diameter. 1 cm (⅜ in) seam allowances have been included.

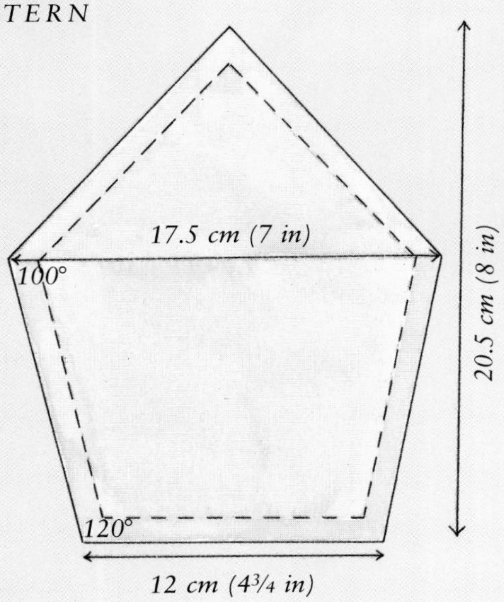

MATERIALS & EQUIPMENT

90 × 20 cm (36 × 8 in) purple velvet
90 × 20 cm (36 × 8 in) maroon velvet
90 × 20 cm (36 × 8 in) green velvet
90 × 15 cm (36 × 6 in) black velvet
90 × 20 cm (36 × 8 in) interfacing
90 × 20 cm (36 × 8 in) black polycotton lining
1 black tassel
black thread

tape measure
dressmakers' grid paper
pencil
paper scissors
dressmakers' pins
dressmaking scissors
sewing machine
needle

SEGMENT PATTERN

17.5 cm (7 in)

100°

120°

20.5 cm (8 in)

12 cm (4¾ in)

Castle hats are made in six sections using three different coloured velvets with a contrast brim, and finished with a pretty tassel. A truly unisex style, a masculine version with a black tassel and a prettier feminine version with a pink tassel are shown here. (*Opposite: Tamsin Young*)

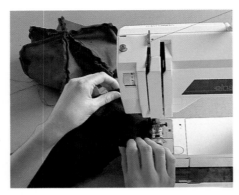

1 With right sides facing, pin a green velvet segment to a purple segment and the other side of the purple segment to a maroon segment. Starting from the centre top, machine down the edge of each segment.

2 Sew the other three segments of the hat as in step 1 and join the two halves together. Place the interfacing on to the wrong side of the velvet hatband. Fold the band in half widthways with right sides facing and sew down the back seam.

3 Fold the hatband in half lengthways and pin it to the main hat piece so that the back seam matches up with one of the segment seams. Pin all the way round.

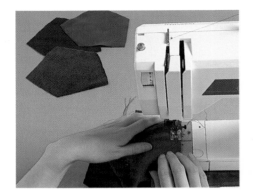

4 Using a straight stitch, machine the band on to the main hat piece. Snip into the corners to allow ease of movement.

5 Sew the tassel by hand to the centre top of the hat.

Note: If the velvet has lost its pile during working, hold it over the steam of a kettle.

6 To make the lining, press the lining circle into quarters. Mark the creases with pins. Fold the lining band in half and machine down the centre back. Place four pins evenly round band. Pleat the band on to the circle, pin into position, matching pins, and sew. Sew the lining into the hat using a hemming stitch.

A collection of fabric dressmakers' hats. Unstructured, soft and with an old-fashioned feel to them, the two at the back are made from silk, one with a large silk bow trim. The one in the foreground is made from velvet with a velvet roses-and-leaves trim. (*Right: Tamsin Young*)

Hand-embroidered bowler

This bowler hat is hand embroidered using tapestry wools. Embroidery threads could be used for a finer effect. Embroidery can be added to almost any bought felt shape or straw hat to add an individual touch. (For the embroidery stitches used in this project, see pages 138–139).

MATERIALS & EQUIPMENT

ready-blocked felt hat
tapestry wools
tailors' chalk or soft pencil

tapestry needle
thimble (optional)
scissors

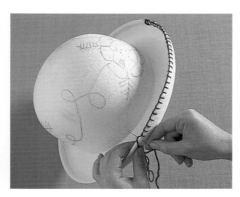

1 Draw the design on to the hat using either pencil or tailors' chalk. Tailors' chalk is easier to rub out if any mistakes are made.

2 Decorate the edge of the brim with blanket stitch. Use the holes made previously by the machine stitching along the edge of the brim. This makes it easier to work out stitch size and therefore gives an even finish.

The navy and black hats show two different colour stories, with a simple repeated flower design embroidered in tapestry wools. The finished project hat is embroidered with a freer overall design. (*Opposite:* white bowler: *Fred Bare;* others: *Monsoon*)

3 Use chain stitch to outline the major shapes such as flowers, and to embroider the tendrils.

4 Fill in the flowers and make leaf shapes in straight stitch. Use French knots to decorate the flower centres, to make them texturally as well as visually interesting.

Summer bonnet

Summer straws come in all styles and they are quick and easy to decorate with ribbons, flowers or straw trim. Suit the embellishment to the shape of the bonnet and the occasion. This old-fashioned-style poke-bonnet with its pretty ribbon, lace and fresh-flower trim would be ideal for a summer bridesmaid teamed with a pretty shepherdess's dress, or to wear to a picnic. Also, if your child has a fancy dress party to attend, follow the project to complete part of a perfect Little Bo Peep costume.

MATERIALS & EQUIPMENT

100 cm (39 in) pink ribbon, 8 cm (3¼ in) wide

fresh flowers and foliage (roses and ivy)

florists' tape

1 cm (⅜ in) edging lace (circumference of bonnet)

straw bonnet

thread

7 cm (2¾ in) wide lace (circumference of bonnet)

ribbon rose-buds

75 cm (29½ in) baby blue ribbon, 8 cm (3¼ in) wide

needle

dressmakers' pins

PREPARATION

Cut the length of pink ribbon in half widthways. Cut a V shape in one end of each piece. This will prevent the ribbon fraying.

Break off any thorns on the rose stems. Crush the ends of the stems and wrap with florists' tape to retain the moisture.

This pretty bonnet derives its charm from the fresh flower and ivy decoration garlanding the crown. If fresh flowers are not available, use dried flowers or fabric flowers or just evergreen foliage. (Opposite)

1   *Sew the narrow lace trim on to the edge of the bonnet.*

2   *Gather the wide lace and draw it up until it measures about three quarters the circumference of the brim.*

3   *Pin the lace into position inside the bonnet so that it starts and finishes about level with the ears, allowing the lace to peep out just beyond the brim. Sew the top edge into position. Sew rose-buds on to the lace at intervals around the brim to prevent the lace flopping on to the face.*

4   *Gather the ribbon ties along the straight ends (without the V). Sew the gathered end on to the sides of the lace and cover the raw edges with more rose-buds.*

5   *Pin the blue ribbon on to the outside of the bonnet and then stab stitch into position. Decorate with a combination of fresh flowers and foliage.*

*F*resh flowers can be tucked easily under a hatband for an immediate decoration. However, use dried or fabric flowers if you want a longer-lasting embellishment. (*Above*)

*F*or a summer bonnet with a more up-to-date look, apply appliqué flowers and leaves made of satin and felt to a plain straw and add a simple hatband. (*Right: Bevali Read*)

Baseball cap

Although known as a baseball cap, this is in fact a version of a cap which is usually made from panels or segments and has a peak. In some countries caps are still occasionally worn as part of a uniform by schoolboys and by cricket teams. The popular American-style baseball cap tends to be brighter and bigger and fits on the head more securely.

PREPARATION

Using the pattern templates on page 141, enlarge on a photocopier by 200%. A seam allowance of 1 cm (³⁄₈ in) has been allowed in the overall dimensions. Cut out the appropriate number of pattern pieces and label accordingly. Press the interfacing on to the wrong side of the fabric, pin the pattern pieces on the bias as shown (see layout plans below and overleaf) and cut out the appropriate pieces for main, contrast and lining fabric.

Cut out the peak from cardboard and brush on three coats of PVA glue to both sides, leaving the glue to dry between coats and between sides.

LAYOUT PLAN A

Contrast fabric/interfacing

B   A   A

Main fabric/interfacing

B   A   A   C

MATERIALS & EQUIPMENT

90 × 50 cm (36 × 20 in) iron-on cotton interfacing
90 × 30 cm (36 × 12 in) yellow (contrast) wool fabric
90 × 50 cm (36 × 20 in) dark red (main) wool fabric
thread
115 × 20 cm (45 × 8 in) lining fabric
14 cm (5½ in) elastic
60 cm (24 in) petersham ribbon

dressmakers' grid paper
pencil
paper scissors
dressmaking scissors
dressmakers' pins
cardboard or plastic peak
PVA glue
glue brush
sewing machine
needle

All these caps are made from the same pattern. The cap in the centre and the black one in the foreground have elongated crown sections which are then caught at the apex to shape them. The hat at right back has earflaps. (*Opposite: Karen Triffitt*)

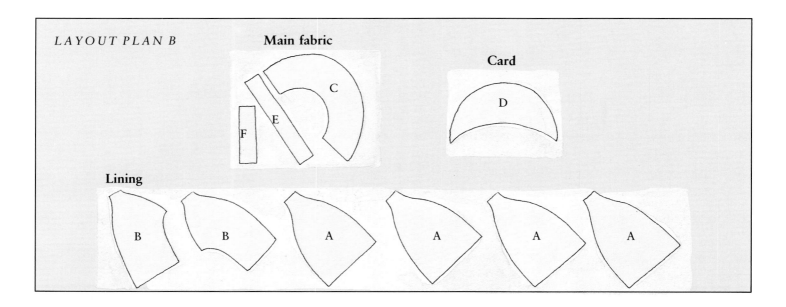

LAYOUT PLAN B

Main fabric

C

E

F

Card

D

Lining

B

B

A

A

A

A

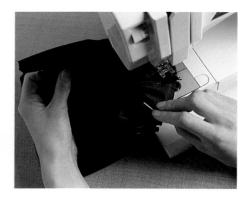

1   *Take the six panels cut from the main and contrast wool fabric (As, Bs). With right sides facing, pin three panels together (A, A, B), alternating the colours. Stitch down the edge of each panel twice, for strength. Repeat with the remaining panels (B, A, A) to produce the two halves of the hat. Snip into the curves to give ease of movement; open out the seams and press them flat.*

2   *Sew the two sections together by pinning the right sides together and sewing from the centre top to one edge and then repeating from the centre top to the other. By sewing this way all the pieces should line up perfectly in the middle. If they do not, it can be disguised by covering a button with matching fabric and sewing this over the join.*

3   *Repeat steps 1 and 2 to make the lining (but without snipping into the curves).*

4 Place the lining inside the crown, wrong sides facing, and sew around the edge 5 mm (¼ in) from the edge. Sew bias strip (E) around the cut-out opening at the back of the hat. Machine stitch 5 mm (¼ in) from the edge, then roll the strip over and hand stitch at the back, as shown.

5 Measure 7 cm (2¾ in) of elastic and mark it, but do not cut. Place the elastic inside the fabric strip (F), and anchor down one end with a couple of stitches. Hand stitch the strip to form a casing. Pull the elastic until the mark reaches the end of the fabric. Secure the elastic at the mark. Cut off the spare elastic and discard.

6 With right sides facing, sew the top of the peak (C with interfacing) to the bottom (C) on the outer curve along the dotted lines. Turn right way out. Place the card shape (D) inside the fabric peak and pull it taut. Baste along the inner curve through both layers, as close to the edge of the card as possible.

7 Matching the centre of the peak with the centre front seam on the cap, sew the peak to the crown, taking, in this instance, a 1.5 cm (⅝ in) seam allowance.

8 Trim this seam allowance to 1 cm (⅜ in), and finish the edge of the cap by overlocking or zigzag stitch all round. Sew in the petersham headband, machining from back to edge of peak on each side, then hand stitch around the front curve.

9 Sew in the covered elastic at the back opening and anchor down the petersham at the sides. Press the petersham on to the inside of the cap all round.

Handmade felt

Felt-making is a very old craft dating back to the ancient Egyptians. The basic techniques of fulling and shaping by hand, refined in medieval times, are still used by village hat makers in some parts of the world, such as Iran and Pakistan. Commercially-produced felt has been used for making hats for centuries and is still a standard material. The method described here is simple, but requires stamina as the wool has to be rolled for at least 25 minutes to mat the fibres together to form felt.

MATERIALS & EQUIPMENT

natural wool coils for the white or undyed base
carded and dyed wool for the top pattern
felt stiffener (optional)
bias binding
thread

towel
beach mat
bucket
warm water
washing-up liquid (detergent)
shallow plastic bowl
elastic bands
dressmaking scissors
needle

PREPARATION

Before shaping the hat, the felt has to be made. Prepare a working area where it doesn't matter if water gets on the floor.

Place the towel on a table and put the beach mat on top of it. Separate the natural wool coils into cotton wool ball (cotton ball) size pieces and start to make a base on the beach mat. Make the base about 30 cm (12 in) square and 5 cm (2 in) thick. Check there are no holes left in the base. Tease out the coloured wool and arrange the design on top of the base (see photograph, above right).

Fill the bucket with warm water and mix in a generous squeeze of washing-up liquid. Sprinkle the wool with the soap mixture and push down the wool making sure all the fibres are thoroughly wet.

Start to roll up the beach mat, enclosing the wool completely. Flip the towel around the beach mat and roll

the mat backwards and forwards as if it were a rolling pin. Do not put a lot of pressure on the mat; it is friction, not pressure, which causes the wool to felt. Roll for about three minutes.

Carefully unroll the mat and turn the felt a quarter turn. Re-roll and continue for five minutes. Repeat the process until the felt has been turned three times. Finally re-roll for five minutes face down.

The simplest of hat shapes to make, yet the brightly coloured felt design makes this creation both vibrant and unusual. This cap would suit men and women equally well. (*Opposite: Anne Marie Cadman*)

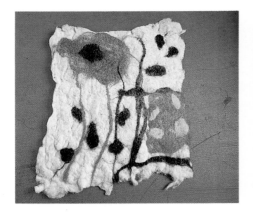

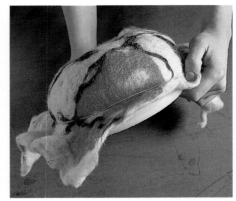

1 When the felt is ready it will be quite thick and the fibres should not move when rubbed with a finger. Don't worry if the edges of the felt seem fragile – they will be cut away when the felt is shaped.

2 Soak the felt in the bucket for a minute and place over the hat mould, in this case a shallow plastic bowl. Place hands on the centre of the felt and push it down so it takes the shape of the mould below it. Put elastic bands over the felt to hold it in place on the mould.

3 When dry, remove the felt and cut off the overlap. The hat may be stiffened with felt stiffener at this stage if preferred, or left with the softer finish. Sew bias binding to the inside rim of the crown. Fold back the binding to the outside of the hat and stitch it by hand covering all raw edges.

These hats are made from knitted and then felted wool, and decorated with rich, intertwining appliqué patterns. (*Left: Teresa Searle*)

A collection of easy-to-wear caps constructed from homemade felts showing a wide range of colour effects. Decorate with a tassel if wished. (*Right: Anne Marie Cadman*)

Waterlily hat

This beautiful, delicate hat can be made from paper or fabric and apart from the brim, which is sewn, the hat is made with origami folds. If using fabric, choose crisp material and iron the folds into place as you construct the hat.

MATERIALS & EQUIPMENT

a perfect square of paper 49.5 × 49.5 cm (19½ × 19½ in)

extra paper to make a brim (this can be as wide as you wish it to be)

thread

tape measure

paper scissors

needle

This version of the waterlily origami hat is in fact made from satin but is folded in the same way as the hat made from paper. (Opposite: Mayling Hung)

Note: *Each step is repeated so that the hat is always symmetrical. Make firm and accurate creases each time a fold is made for a crisp and neat finish.*

1   *Fold the paper diagonally. Fold in half and unfold.*

2   *With the open corner at the top, open out one half of the triangle and fold down the hypotenuse so that one 45° angle meets the other. Turn over and repeat, lining up the four open corners carefully, to form a diamond shape.*

3   *With the open corner on the top, fold the side corners into the centre as shown. Repeat on the reverse side.*

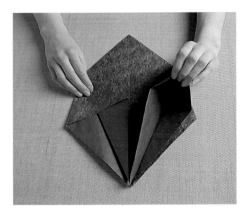

4 Lift up the flaps made in step 3, open out and crease to form upside-down kite shapes. Repeat on all four flaps.

5 Fold the four kite shapes in half, tucking the outside edges behind the inner edges. The finished shape resembles another upside-down kite (see step 6).

6 Fold down the four peaks individually.

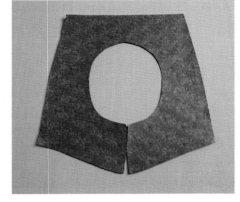

7 The crown of the hat is formed by opening up the shape.

8 Measure the circumference of your head for the centre of the brim and add a 1 cm (³⁄₈ in) seam allowance. Cut a brim with a dart in the centre back. This will allow the hat to dip slightly at the back.

9 Sew the dart in the centre back and attach the brim to the crown. Trim any odd corners off the crown.

Machine-embroidered hat

These wonderful hats are machine-embroidered over the whole surface and are very rich in design and feel. Each hat tells a story and because the hats are round, the story goes on forever. All the embroidered designs are figurative, with delicate, humorous images depicting story-lines of situations and events, naive and mythical. Experiment with designs of your own, using geometric patterns for simplicity.

MATERIALS & EQUIPMENT

90 × 120 cm (36 × 47 in) medium-weight calico
sewing thread (silk rayon was used here as it has a lovely sheen)
90 × 25 cm (36 × 10 in) lining fabric (checked silk dupion was used here)

pencil
sewing machine with a darning foot
embroidery hoop
scissors

PREPARATION

If you are using a domestic sewing machine, the machine will need to rest every so often to stop the motor overheating. Before you begin, it is a good idea to practise machine embroidery on a spare piece of calico, to get the feel of the technique and to work out the tension you will need to use. Drop the feed dog-teeth on the machine. Turn the stitch length to 0 and the width to 0. With machine embroidery the fabric is moved backwards and forwards by the use of an embroidery frame which is why you do not need a stitch length. Hold the fabric taut in the embroidery hoop and work from the middle outwards, moving the frame to fill in each area. Practise the technique and adjust the tension as necessary.

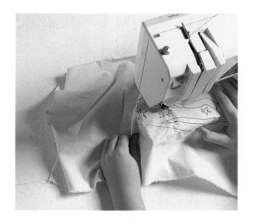

Note: *the measurements for the calico in the materials listing includes a 15–20 cm (6–8 in) border around the band and crown to allow for working.*

1 *Mark a band 62.5 cm (24½ in) long × 11 cm (4¼ in) deep on to calico. (When the band is embroidered it should be about 61 cm (24 in) long.) Draw the design in pencil and then with the feed dog-teeth in their normal position sew over the pencil outline using a normal running stitch.*

Mark a 20 cm (8 in) diameter circle on the calico for the crown and draw in the design as you did for the band above. (When the crown is fully embroidered it will measure 19.5 cm (7½ in).) Place the calico in the embroidery hoop. When the outlines of the design have been stitched, prepare the machine for machine embroidery.

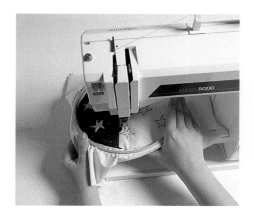

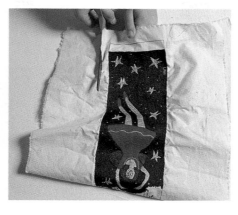

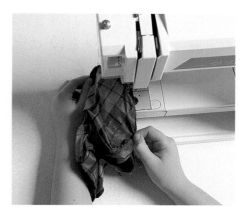

2 Fill in the design as if colouring a painting, not forgetting to rest the machine when it gets hot. The machine embroidery will appear to shrink the material. If this happens too much embroider a little more fabric at the sides. Work the crown of the hat in the same way as the band.

3 Once the design is filled in cut out the embroidery band and crown leaving a 5 mm (¼ in) seam allowance all the way round.

4 Sew the crown and band together as for the Smoking Cap project (see pages 26–29).
    When the outer hat is complete, measure and cut a lining to the same dimensions. Sew the lining band to the lining crown.

*T*hree traditionally shaped hats decorated with machine embroidery: the two at the front depict flowers while the hat at the back features cave-painting-type figures. (*Right: Fred Bare*)

*T*hese hats are machine-embroidered over the whole surface using shiny rayon threads and whimsical figurative imagery for a unique finish. (*Left: Linda Miller*)

5 With the wrong sides facing, insert the lining into the outer hat. Catch with a stitch in the middle of the crown and then turn under all seams and slip stitch the lining into place around the edge of the hat.

Fake-fur hat

This very stylish hat can be made with a deep crown and worn like a top hat or it may be pinned or gathered on one side and worn as something a little less daring but more elegant. As with all dressmakers' hats the fabric must be cut on the bias to allow for stretch and a good fit over the head. Fake-fur fabric is available in many weights, qualities and patterns. Choose the best quality affordable.

PREPARATION

Using the pattern templates on page 140, enlarge on a photocopier by 400%. A seam allowance of 1.5 cm (⅝ in) has been allowed in the overall dimensions. Cut out the appropriate number of pattern pieces and label.

Place the interfacing on the wrong side of the fur fabric and pin the pattern pieces into place (see layout plan below) and cut through both layers. Place pattern pieces D and E on the lining fabric, pin and cut out.

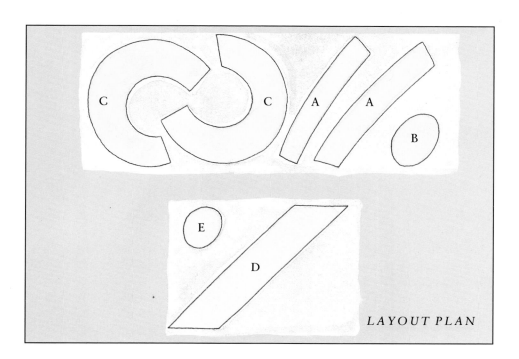

LAYOUT PLAN

MATERIALS & EQUIPMENT

140 × 50 cm (55 × 20 in) interfacing (stiffened muslin (cheesecloth) was used here)

140 × 50 cm (55 × 20 in) fake-fur fabric

70 × 50 cm (28 × 20 in) lining fabric

thread

60 cm (23½ in) petersham ribbon 2.5 cm (1 in) wide

dressmakers' grid paper

pencil

paper scissors

dressmakers' pins

dressmaking scissors

sewing machine

needle

The project hat is made of good-quality thick fake-fur fabric which gives the hat form. The same pattern has been used for the hat at right back, but it is made from thinner fur for a softer, less structured shape. The black and white fake Friesian fur is made with only one part of the sideband for a lower crown. (*Opposite: Karen Triffitt*)

1 First make the lining. Fold the band (D) in half widthways with right sides facing and sew back seam. Press open the seam. Pin pleats into place along the top edge. With right sides facing, pin the band on to the tip (E) and adjust as necessary, removing the previous set of pins at the same time. Machine into place using a straight stitch. Remove the pins.

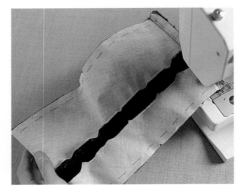

2 With right sides facing, sew the two crown pieces (A,A) together along the dotted lines. Open out the seam by hand and cut notches evenly along both seam allowances. Join the back seam together and open out the seam allowance. Cut a notch at the join of the two seams. Snip along the top edge at even intervals to a depth of 5 mm (¼ in).

3 With right sides facing, pin tip (B) to the wider part of band (A) (where it was previously snipped). The snipping will allow the band to be eased on to the tip. Machine, removing the pins, and trim the seam allowances to 1 cm (⅜ in). Turn right side out.

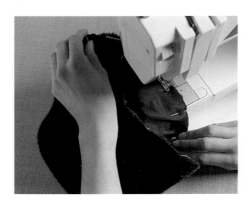

4 With the wrong sides facing, place the lining inside the crown and machine into place 5 mm (¼ in) from the edge.

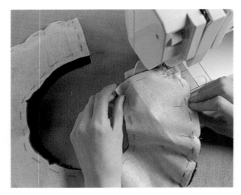

5 To make the brim sew the two brim pieces (C) together, with right sides facing, along the outer edge. Trim the seam allowance to 1 cm (⅜ in). Open out seam allowance.

6 Open out the two brim pieces that have been sewn together. Pin the two ends together and sew the back seam of the brim. Open out the seam allowance, and make notches at the join of the two seams.

7   *Turn the brim the right way out, and sew the front and back together 1 cm (³/₈ in) in from the edge. Snip along this edge at even intervals.*

8   *With the right side of the crown and the top side of the brim together, sew the crown to the brim. Finish the edge by overlocking or zigzag stitch.*

9   *Sew in the petersham ribbon along the same row of stitching.*

Tip: When sewing fur fabric try to make the pile lie away from the line of stitching. Pull out any fur which has caught in the stitching with a pin.

Appliquéd garland brim

This delicate hat is very pretty and unusual in that it doesn't have a crown. The techniques involved in the making include dyeing, blocking, appliqué and sewing. The appliqué flowers can also be made to decorate a ready-blocked straw hat; or vary the materials to embellish a winter felt.

MATERIALS & EQUIPMENT

green cold-water dye
fine white straw capeline hood
white petersham ribbon
pearled lamé
yellow and purple velvet
purple ready-purchased or handmade felt
wadding
purple and shot orange silk
iridescent green organza
purple chiffon
thread

needle
dressmaking scissors
kettle
wooden head block
drawing pins
sewing machine
millinery wire (optional)
dressmakers' pins

PREPARATION

The straw hood can be stiffened after dyeing but it is not necessary. If the materials detailed here cannot be found, use other luxury fabrics instead.

If you want to experiment with handmade felt, follow the basic instructions for the Handmade Felt project.

1 Dye the straw and the ribbon according to the dye manufacturer's instructions. Cut out the crown of the hood 5 cm (2 in) down from the tip and steam the whole of the straw under the spout of a kettle. To begin, concentrate on stretching the head fitting.

2 Secure the head fitting on to the head block using drawing pins, and leave it to dry.

Called a hat, but in fact only a brim, this is a lovely creation to wear on a not-too-hot summer's day. It is made from dyed straw and decorated with appliquéd silk and felt flowers, buds and berries. (*Opposite: Abigail Mill*)

3   Machine or hand stitch the headband to the inside of the crown and neaten the outside edge of the crown by machine stitching.

4   Appliqué flowers of pearled lamé and yellow velvet on to the felt and cut them out.

5   Make berries in various sizes by wrapping balls of wadding in pieces of velvet, silk and organza and tying them with thread. Wrap the larger berries with silk and organza to form buds.

These four hats each use appliqué in a different way. Clockwise from left back: a lace-covered hat with a green velvet brim and hatband decorated with pearlized appliqué. The felt bowler has a round brim and shell-like appliqué has been applied as a band between the brim and the crown.

The straw hat has a wavy brim and is appliquéd with ribbon and balls of silk. The green bowler is made from silk and velvet and covered with iridescent appliqué 'peacock-tail' designs. (*Right: Abigail Mill*)

6   Gather a strip of green organza and one of purple chiffon so they are long enough to drape around the crown. Pin the strips into position on the base of the crown.

7   Sew the flowers and berries on to the chiffon and organza trim. To achieve a more rigid edge to the brim, it could be finished with millinery wire.

Decorating a felt

Although a felt hat with a distinctive upturned brim has been chosen for this embellishment, the basic method can be adapted to decorate any style of hat. This hat has already been blocked. If bought from a chain store a blocked felt hat may already have a hatband and head fitting. These can be removed and replaced with new materials, if wished.

Decorated with a draped red velvet trim around the crown, a feather cockade and a covered-button trim, this plain black felt has been totally transformed.

PREPARATION

It is easy to make a feather cockade by binding single feathers and sewing them together to form a fan shape.

MATERIALS & EQUIPMENT

black felt hat
petersham ribbon for headband
thread
90 × 100 cm (36 × 40 in) red velvet to make 'sausage' (see step 1 for dimensions)
button kit for covered button
feather trim

needle
dressmaking scissors
sewing machine
dressmakers' pins

1 Sew the headband into the hat by hand. Make a 'sausage' by cutting on the bias a piece of fabric 1½ times the circumference of the crown by twice the depth. With right sides together, fold the fabric in half lengthways and machine along the long edge.

2 Turn the sausage the right way round and start to pin it on to the crown at the appropriate place where you wish to finish. This may be at the side or the back of the hat depending on the design. Arrange the sausage in pleats and folds and pin in place.

3 Finish with a twist which will hide all the raw edges and ends. Sew the sausage shape into position, holding the headband down and out of the way so as not to catch it with the stitches. Sew the feather cockade to the sausage and cover the end with the covered button.

$\mathcal{H}$ATS FOR EVERY OCCASION

Hats can be worn to make a fashion statement, as a practical protection against hot or cold weather, and often simply because a particular occasion 'demands' it. This chapter looks at the types of hat you might like to wear for any of these reasons. There are easy-to-wear hats for children and traditional and fashionable ideas to tempt men into head gear; smart hats for weddings, christenings and other special occasions, and pert and frivolous cocktail hats for parties. There are holiday hats for those free and easy days of relaxation in both hot and cold climates, and some wonderfully eclectic and outrageous creations for the bold. Hints and tips are given so you can recreate some of these hats at home, either the hat in its entirety or the trimmings and embellishments which can then be used to adapt a hat you have already.

Smart hats

Nearly everyone at some time or another will want to wear a smart hat to complete an outfit – for a wedding or christening, perhaps. Sometimes, strict dress codes literally demand that one be worn!

The pink straw with a brim covered in pink ostrich feathers is a very feminine hat. The brim of the cream straw hat has a wavy edge and is decorated with tiny pearl beads. (*Left:* from top: *Bevali Read, Karen Triffitt*)

The pale straw is trimmed with gauzy fabric knotted over the crown. The cone-shaped hat is covered with two toning colours of petals. The classy black straw has a simple brown bow trim. (*Right:* from top: *Viv Knowland, Lucy Barlow, Lucy Barlow*)

Smart hats are formal: they may have a romantic air with large brims swathed in soft, transparent and gauzy fabrics or they may feature crisp colour combinations such as navy/cream or emerald green/navy or purple/fuchsia pink. Wide-brimmed hats are often graceful and elegant, but smaller shapes are easier to carry off if you are not a regular hat wearer. If buying a special occasion hat always try it on with the outfit with which it is to be worn. If you love the shape and basic colour, do not worry if the trim is wrong as this is one area that can be easily changed to personalize the hat. Check that the hat is in proportion so that no one part of the outfit dwarfs the rest. Lastly, practise wearing the hat so you don't feel self-conscious on the day.

Model hats – as the millinery equivalent of couturier clothes are known – are hand-made and sewn and specially fitted to a client, hence the expense. However, if such prices are beyond you, make your own smart hat by buying a simple straw or felt and embellishing it exactly as you wish.

These two hats are extremely elegant. The black straw brimmed hat is topped with a white slub silk, enlarged crown. The black straw picture hat is decorated with black ostrich feathers and turquoise fabric roses. (*Right: Bevali Read, Herald and Heart Hatters*)

To make Organdie petals

PREPARATION

These organdie petals can be adapted in several ways. To turn them into flowers, gather the petals at the base and sew several together. For an open flower, cut smaller petals to surround the centre of the flower for a more realistic effect. Fabric-covered buttons are ideal for flower centres. Instead of rolling the edges of the petals, cut petals through a double thickness of fabric and pin them together with right sides facing and then sew around the edge using a running stitch. Turn through to the right side and add definition to the shape by top stitching near the edge, if wished.

1 Cut a cardboard petal-shaped template. Position the template on the white organdie so it lies across the bias of the fabric. Draw round the shape and cut out as many petals as you require. Pull each petal to stretch.

This stylish yet feminine daisy hat would grace any special occasion. The white organdie petals are very easy to make; simply follow the instructions. To make a similar hat, cover the brim of a low-crowned straw hat with the petals and then cover the crown with four larger petals made of green silk. A rolled silk stalk completes the picture.
(*Left: Ellen Bonner*)

2   Moisten your finger and thumb in a bowl of water and begin to roll the edges of the petal.

3   Take care to keep the smooth line of the edge as you roll and keep your fingers damp. Repeat with all the petals.

4   Attach the top point of each petal to the hat, building up several overlapping layers.

*T*wo hats ideal for the season: a burnt-orange silk picture hat and a daisy hat with petals made from organdie in green and white covering a straw base. (*Above:* from left: *Herald and Heart Hatters, Ellen Bonner*)

Cocktail hats

Here are three stunning cocktail hats, typified by the small basic shape and glitzy trimmings. Clockwise from left: a red velvet-covered buckram with large felt leaves wired down the centre to give them body; nets, feathers and beaded trim embellish a simple shape; a dramatic black and white hat with a tall ostrich feather.
(*Left: Herald and Heart Hatters*)

The ultimate cocktail hat, this has everything – glitz, froth and dazzle. The veil adds mystery, and allows the black metallic straw to show through but not dominate. It is finished with a bead and feather trim.
(*Right: Herald and Heart Hatters*)

A cocktail hat has no practical function (it will certainly not protect you from inclement weather) but it will get you noticed. And with that aim in mind, it should be a frivolous and witty creation, small in shape and worn perched on top of the head and carried with confidence. Wearing a ritzy cocktail hat takes preparation: dress up to the nines, put up your hair, sweep it back with gel or choose an old-fashioned set hairstyle with lots of curls and lacquer. For an enticing effect, tilt the hat forward at an angle over the forehead. A face veil adds a hint of mystery.

Cocktail hats are fairly easy to make (see the project on pages 30–33), as the basic head shapes are simple. Cover a straw or buckram shape with rich material (silks, satins, velvets, shot organza) and then run riot with stiffened or gathered net, feathers, beads and lace trimmings. The hats shown here should provide ample inspiration.

A deep-crowned velvet cocktail hat with a pretty, stylized daisy top.
(*Top: Herald and Heart Hatters*)

T hese fun musical-instrument cocktail hats are made from card and wired buckram covered with velvet, silk and felt.
(*Above: Lucy Barlow*)

Holiday hats

If you are in a hot country, a hat is essential for keeping off the sun. Summer hats are usually made of straw, and a simple straw can be twisted, dyed, curled and adapted to suit the holiday mood. Decorate a straw or cotton hat with pebbles or shells picked up from the beach, or use a colourful cotton scarf as a hatband. Use local flowers, dried herbs or even weeds to decorate a brim — and perhaps even change the decoration daily to suit your mood and clothes.

This cloche-shaped cap is made from felted wool decorated with a fringe and unusual figurative imagery. This is an ideal style for outdoor winter sports such as skiing or ice skating.
(*Right: Tait and Style*)

Winter holiday hats should keep you warm, but they do not have to be boring. They can be decorated with brooches, badges or embroidery. For skiing, customize wool hats with appliqué or pom-poms — or wear an old leather flying cap; either way you will stand out from the crowd.

The ultimate holiday hat with net, appliquéd fabric fish, and shells – just add your own seaweed! (*Left: Herald and Heart Hatters*)

Three holiday hats. The hat at top is made from plaited straw and simply decorated with a straw plait around the crown. At bottom left is a cheeky holiday hat with a ribbon tie at the side. On the right, a Fifties-style coolie hat. (*Above: Herald and Heart Hatters*)

*T*wo laid-back foxy hats made from dyed sisal with voile hatbands and trimmed with fabric flowers dyed to match. Perfect for a summer holiday, wear them casually with T-shirts or dress them up with a simple summer frock.
(*Above: Gil Fox*)

And when on holiday don't forget to buy a hat from the country you are visiting – not a tourist hat but the genuine article, a Turkish fez, Mexican sombrero, French beret, American stetson or whatever. Moreover, wear the hat when you return home; berets, for example, can be worn with practically anything or a fez could be teamed with wide-legged trousers and an embroidered waistcoat.

To decorate a Holiday hat

Create a new holiday hat by decorating the crown and brim of a plain straw with stencilled designs. Wax stencil crayons were used as the stencilling medium here; they are easy to apply and don't smudge or cause a mess. A fabric hatband (actually a length of recycled haberdashery trim) in toning colours completes the transformation. (*Left*)

A very beautiful, delicate summer straw; the edges of the wavy brim are dyed so that the colours change from rose pink through orange to a soft yellow, merging into the cream colour of the crown. The rose trim features the same use of gradated colour and is also formed from straw. (*Left: Bailey and Tomlin*)

1 Rub the wax crayon on the edge of the stencil and then coat the brush with the wax colour. Dab the brush on to the hat through the first stencil.

2 Leave to dry for 3 to 4 hours before applying the next colour with the second stencil. Repeat until all the colours have been applied.

Children's hats

As we lose between thirty and forty per cent of body heat from the head it is important that we keep our heads covered in winter. This is particularly vital for babies and children. Equally, in summer protect children from the sun with cool, lightweight and wide-brimmed hats.

Children look great in hats but it is often difficult to persuade a young child to wear one for more than a few minutes. Most important is to make sure the hat is the correct size and not too heavy; if the hat is uncomfortable they'll never wear it! Be devious, and make the hat part of a character he or she is interested in: a summer straw may become a sailor's hat, or a princess's bonnet; a felt can become a pirate or cowboy hat. Make a child's hat interesting by adding appliqué or bead work in animal shapes, or embroider eyes and a smiling mouth on the top of a beret. For a little girl who is interested in being pretty, decorate a straw boater with flowers, lace and ribbons; or liven-up a boring old school hat with bright embroidery or pom-poms. For spring and summer bridesmaids, choose simple garlands made of dried or fresh flowers wired to a fabric-covered headband; or dried leaves and berries for autumn and winter weddings.

*T*wo unusual coronets for bridesmaids. The head-dress on the left is made from hand-painted silk, formed into two 'sausages' and filled with wadding. They are then twisted together and decorated with very narrow ribbon, strings of fake pearls and pretty glass beads. The other coronet is made from fused appliqué, machine embroidery and bits of metal. (*Right:* metallic coronet: *Judy Clayton*)

*C*hildren's fabric berets are classic in style and can be worn unadorned or trimmed with a feather hat pin. Add a black and white ribbon to the headband for a nautical look. (*Above*)

*T*hese pretty straw children's hats have been dyed and then trimmed with a simple paper flower or a string to tie under the chin. They are light and easy to wear – perfect for kids. (*Above and right: Gil Fox*)

To decorate a Child's hat

For a simple but attractive child's hat, take a plain straw or cotton sailor hat and decorate with seashell buttons and beached starfish. This idea can be endlessly adapted: exchange the sailor hat for a soft felt, and decorate with colourful animal-shaped buttons, for example. (Left)

1 *Sew the various shell buttons round the base of the crown.*

2 *Simply glue the starfish to the top of the hat.*

M *en's hats*

A man's boater could be worn with a fashionable pigtail and a Breton shirt, or an Eton crop and a navy blazer – this hat looks good whatever your style. (*Right: Herbert Johnson*)

Traditional men's hats such as trilbies, Panamas, top hats and bowlers have always had their adherents, despite the demise in hat wearing over the past forty years, and still look very stylish today. Hats for men are once again becoming popular however and they are being designed and worn in a much freer way than before. Designers such as Fred Bare have, for instance, taken the traditional and distinctive

T raditional summer hats for men include peaked caps, boaters and Panamas. Three types of Panama are shown here. In the wooden box is a Montecristi fino – the Rolls Royce of Panamas. The classic folding Panama, rolled in its case, has a trademark central ridge across the crown. A standard Panama shows the typical dipped and pinched crown. (*Right: Herbert Johnson*)

A collection of men's winter hats made from felts, with the flat cap being made from wool. These classic styles look as good today on the modern man as they did on his father and grandfather in the early decades of this century. (*Left: Herbert Johnson*)

shapes of the bowler and trilby and embroidered them with flowers and animals! Nineteenth-century smoking caps are reappearing in richly coloured silks, topped with tassels. Tweedy flat-caps and jaunty peaked caps are a perennial favourite, and can be found in traditional and bright colourways. These hats do not merge into the background, and are worn by both men and women. So, if you want to wear a masculine-style hat – wear a man's hat. They look better than an imitation version.

A traditional felt looks stylish, keeps off the rain and might get you a job as a private detective! (*Left: Herbert Johnson*)

*A*man's smoking cap, so called in the nineteenth century as it was worn to prevent the hair smelling of tobacco. Great head gear for any fashion-conscious man – or woman.
(*Below: Herbert Johnson*)

*T*his richly patterned top hat is for the snazzy dresser who wants to be noticed, and is a welcome change from the traditional black or grey topper.
(*Right: Herbert Johnson*)

*M*en's brightly coloured jockey caps, made in pure wool, look great on girls, too. (*Right: Herbert Johnson*)

*F*or those of you who wouldn't think of decorating men's hats here are some ideas to change your mind. Decorate with a feather or two, or strap a leather belt with a good brass buckle around the crown. Alternatively, tie an elegant dressing-gown cord round a stiff upper-crust bowler or a printed bandana round a straw Panama. (*Left*)

Novelty hats

Novelty hats might be worn for any of the occasions or purposes already described, but they warrant a section of their own because they are so different. Frequently made of unconventional hat materials they are also often made to look like something other than a hat. They are bright, bold, unusual in form and utterly individual.

These very beautiful and unusual hats are all made from natural materials including husks, seaweed, dried leaves, grasses and twigs. The hat bases are formed from spartre and coloured with spray paint and the natural decorations have been bleached and dyed.
(*Below: Sharon Mitchell*)

A Tower Bridge hat made from a sponge base covered with felt and decorated with velvet and gold cords. (*Right: Bevali Read*)

The designs featured here include hats decorated with seaweed, husks, and shells, a rainhat made from recycled plastic bags, and even a millinery rendition of Tower Bridge. Let your imagination run riot and use anything to hand for your own whacky creations. The only restriction is don't use materials which will make the hat too heavy to wear.

A wonderful collection of straw crowns, made of conventional straw hoods and straw trims but used in a very imaginative way. (*Left: Victoria Brown*)

This crown is made from two felt hoods; the magenta hood is placed inside a red one and then decorated with green felt trims; the edges are rolled and embroidered. (*Right: Gil Fox*)

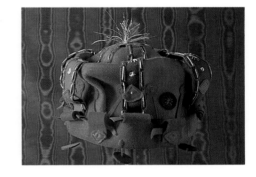

These three crowns are made of handmade blocked felt. The richly coloured crowns are decorated with felt shapes, and the black crown with pin heads and mirrors, inspired by the maker's trip to India. (*Left: Victoria Brown*)

*T*his cone-shaped hat is covered with layers of fabric petals in many shades of green. (*Below: Bevali Read*)

A rainhat made from recycled plastic bags. The fabric is made from squares of cut-up bags which are top stitched and then used to make the hat. (*Above: Karen Triffitt*)

A fuchsia hat; the petals are made from wired spartre covered with cotton and silk. (*Right: Wendy Watt*)

To make a Papier-mâché hat

Create a stir with this brightly coloured hat made from papier-mâché – ideal for fancy dress parties. It's great fun to make; the basic hat shape can be changed by using different moulds and the decorative possibilities are endless.

1 Choose a cake tin a little larger than the required head size. Grease the inside of the tin with petroleum jelly to lubricate it. Line the tin with layers of paper soaked in a mixture of two parts PVA glue to one part water. Leave the paper to dry between coats. Apply six coats in all.

2 Remove the papier-mâché mould from the tin and brush with white emulsion paint.

3 Make papier-mâché roses from strips of paper dipped in glue, folded in half lengthways and then curled to make a rose shape. Make the stems from wire ties or garden wire and cover with paper.

4 Paint the roses and the hat with designers' gouache and allow to dry. Stick the decorations to the hat with impact adhesive.

EMBELLISHING HATS

The embellishment or trim is often what gives a hat that spark of originality, and as you will see from the photographs throughout the book you can trim a hat with almost anything. Moreover, a treasured hat can be revitalized by simply removing faded and dusty trims and replacing them with something new. Here we describe some traditional and more unusual embellishments, from beautiful silk roses and varied ribbon trims to sparkling beads and sequins and feminine hats and veils. The materials need not be expensive: you can recycle fabric remnants and pieces of haberdashery such as cording, fringing and decorative braiding. Follow the simple step-by-step sequences for making a wide range of decorations.

Hat pins

These dazzling hat pins combine machine embroidery and appliqué with metalwork. (*Right: Judy Clayton*)

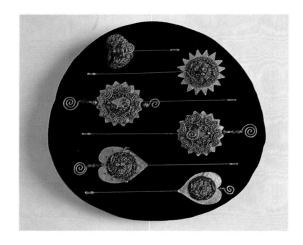

Hat pins may seem to be an anachronism today but they are a pretty adornment to a wide range of hats. They may have originated as hair pins, with the pin passing through both the hat and the hair to anchor the hat firmly into position. When they were first used towards the end of the nineteenth century, hat pins were about 12.5 cm (5 in) long, much as they are today. As hat styles changed, so did the pins, until some were as long as 28 cm (11 in). This suited the style of early twentieth-century hats which were large and worn perched on top of the typically bouffant hairstyles of the Edwardian era. Unlike the pins of today they were not equipped with safety nibs to guard the points; they often stuck out dangerously and even caused bodily damage as one report in a 1913 edition of *The New York Times* relates. A young man was off work for two weeks

and scarred for life after being damaged by a hat pin while travelling on the Brooklyn elevated train!

Almost anything can be attached to a hat pin to add decoration to an otherwise plain hat: feathers and beads, ribbons and cords, and miniature flowers, musical instruments or animals made of metals, wood or bone, for example.

To make a Beaded hat pin

A selection of hat pins featuring beads, feathers, sequins, metallic leaves and tassels shows the infinite variety available for every hat and each occasion. (*Below: Penny Pins*; velvet rosette hat pin: *Tamsin Young*)

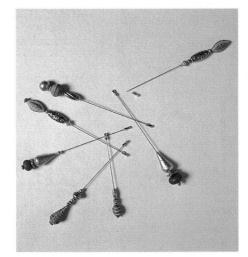

*B*y varying the colours and shapes of the beads, these hat pins can be made to complement many different styles of hat in all colourways.

MATERIALS & EQUIPMENT

lapel pin with safety end
various beads
crimping bead

pair of flat-nosed jewellers' pliers

1 Remove the safety end from the lapel pin and experiment with various arrangements of the beads until you have a pleasing composition.
  Thread the beads on in the correct order.

2 Thread on the crimping bead. Push all the beads up to the head end of the pin, then squeeze the crimping bead with the flat-nosed pliers.

Handmade flowers

Roses are classic and popular hat embellishments, and can be made from many different materials to any size required.

Although it is possible to make fabric flowers the time involved is probably not worth while as there are so many comparatively inexpensive fabric and paper flowers available to buy. One exception to this are fabric roses which are easy to make and can be fashioned in a wide range of fabrics to match any given outfit (see overleaf, To Make a Fabric Rose). The other exception are large petals which may be made from organdie (see pages 80–81).

Bought flowers can be made from many materials including plastic and paper, and fabrics such as silk, velvet, satin, organdie or polyester. The variety in style and size of artificial flowers is too vast to mention in detail as they vary from the tiniest clusters of miniature forget-me-nots to large over-blown roses.

You may find that sometimes the stems and greenery on cheap flowers are rather poor. Rejuvenate by rewiring on to linen-covered stem wire, or wrap in florists' tape or cover with bias binding.

If making your own flower and leaf accessories, most of the components can be bought separately and joined together to create individual designs. Use binding wire to hold small bunches of stems, petals and leaves together. Items such as tiny stamens and berries are also available and these can be used to create realistic or fantasy flowers depending on the effect required.

Always experiment with flower trims, for while one hat may look fine with a single flower another hat may need something extra – perhaps several flowers grouped together or one flower arranged with grasses, chiffon or ribbon.

These three hats show the varied ways in which hats can be decorated with flowers. The vibrant orange straw is decorated with fabric flowers dyed to match the hatband. The natural straw is decorated with an unusual flower trim made from brown wrapping paper. The open-mesh straw is decorated with appliqué flowers; buttons covered in red silk are used as flower centres.
(*Right:* clockwise from top: *Gil Fox, Viv Knowland, Bevali Read*)

To make a Fabric rose

Purchase a plain straw hat from a
department store. Cover the
crown and brim with veiling and baste
into position through the straw. Sew on
handmade silk roses around the crown.
Add another lace veil to cover the hat
completely, including the roses.
(*Meryl Lloyd*)

PREPARATION

*The amount of fabric you need
depends on the size and fullness of the
bloom. A small bud will take much less
fabric than a full-blown rose. If making
a fairly stiff rose with flimsy fabric,
iron on a webbing backing to add
strength. When cutting fabric, unless
using ribbon with a bound edge or felt
which is non-fraying, choose a fabric
twice the depth (plus seam allowance)
of the finished rose.*

1 *With right sides facing, fold the
fabric in half and sew one end
together using neat running stitches.
Turn the fabric the right way round so
the stitches are hidden.*

2 *Keeping the ribbon folded in half
down its length, and starting with
the stitched end, roll the fabric three or
four times to form the centre of the
rose. Secure at the base with a few
running stitches.*

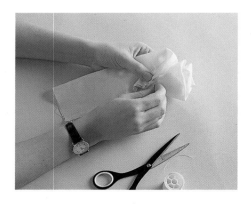

3 *To form petals, roll the fabric so
it is wider at the top. The best
way to do this is to gather the fabric at
the base and secure with small stitches
as you turn it. You may wish to fold the
top edge of the fabric to give a more
authentic look to the petals.*

4 *To finish, tuck the raw edges of
the fabric in and fold the
neatened edge back. Secure with more
stitches. It is not important that the
underneath of the rose is untidy as it
will be hidden when the rose is sewn to
the hat.*

R *ibbons*

Ribbons come in a wide variety of materials, widths, colourways and textures. They may be stiff or floppy, woven or printed, geometric or floral in design, and they may have a watermarked or grosgrained finish or a decorative picot edging. The most popular ribbon for embellishing hats is petersham, which is used for making headbands, hatbands and trims.

Fitting a ribbon hatband snugly around a crown is an art. It looks simple but it is difficult to achieve a smooth, unpuckered finish. If you are using a petersham ribbon, you will find that it has a great deal of give which is useful. However, not all ribbons give in the same way and they may benefit from being steamed and stretched with a warm iron. For some ribbons such as velvet or satin it may be necessary to have a twist half-way round the crown or to shape the ribbon into a V at a point where it can be covered with a trim.

*T*hree richly decorated hats. The top one uses a combination of brown ribbons made from different materials to give an interesting visual and tactile finish. The trim on the red hat shows a way of extending a small exquisite piece of material by joining it to a wide ribbon in a complementary colour. The black hat on the left uses a wide ribbon decorated with a straw trim. (*Right: Herald and Heart Hatters*)

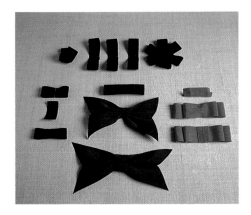

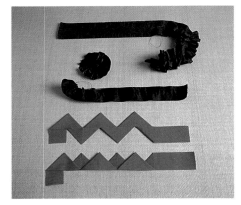

Four simple ribbon trims. Clockwise from top: flat rosette; double bow; gathered bow; single bow. The photograph shows the component parts for each trim and the finished effect.

Three ribbon trims. From top: a simple gathered hatband; gathered rosette; triangular trim.

Tie bow
This is a soft, very full bow and can be made with large loops and ends for a dramatic effect. One length of ribbon is needed. Fold one end under to form the first loop. Then fold the second end into a similar loop; pass the first loop in front of the second and through the centre twist. Pull both loops to adjust.

Single bow
The size of the finished bow will depend on the width of the ribbon, so choose narrow ribbon for a small bow and wide ribbon for a fuller shape. Make one ribbon loop, then wrap a piece of ribbon about half the length of the loop around the midpoint and stitch at the back.

Double bow
This is made in the same way as a single bow, but using two loops of

ribbon, one slightly larger than the first. Sew one on top of the other before covering the join with a small plain or pleated ribbon band.

Gathered bow
Cut an oblong piece of ribbon the size you require for the finished bow, and cut a narrow piece of ribbon about half the length of the larger piece. Cut V shapes into the two ends of the large piece of ribbon, then make a line of running stitch down the midpoint; gather and knot the end of the thread to hold. Wrap the narrow ribbon over the midpoint to cover the gather. Tuck the ends under and stitch in place.

Flat rosette
To make this simple rosette trim, you will need four ribbon loops of equal length. Place three loops one on top of the other to form a star shape and

stitch in the centre. Twist the fourth loop and sew on top of the rosette to cover the join.

Gathered rosette
Gather a length of ribbon down one long edge with little running stitches. Ease the ribbon into a circle, overlap the two ends slightly and neaten. Cover the centre of the rosette with a button covered in the same ribbon fabric, or in a contrasting colour.

Pleated trim
Petersham can be pleated to form a decorative trim for a hatband or edge. The pleating needs to be crisp and sharp to look smart. The width of each pleat should not be more than the width of the ribbon. As a rough guide for a band or a brim trim you will need three times the finished length in ribbon. Use the ribs in petersham as a guide for folding. Form all the pleats for the full length, making sure they are even, and baste them into place. For a band, catch them in the folds and stab stitch along the centre.

Triangular trim
For this you will need a long length of ribbon and an iron. Fold the ribbon so that triangles are formed alternately top and bottom and back and front of the centre line. Iron each triangle as you form it. When the ribbon is completely made up of triangles, bring the bottom ones up to the centre line and iron them flat. You will now have a line of slightly overlapping triangles. Cut the trim to fit around the crown and attach using stab stitch.

To make a Ribbon cockade

*E*asy to sew, this black ribbon cockade trim complements the brim binding and offers a good colour contrast to the simply shaped red felt hat.

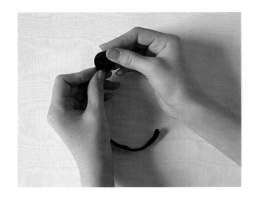

1 *Fold a narrow piece of petersham in half lengthways and roll. Catch the end with a few stitches.*

2 *Pleat a wider piece of petersham into a circle, catching the pleats at the centre with a few stitches as you go to stop it unwinding.*

3 *Stitch the cockade to the hat.*

4 *Finally, sew the roll of petersham (made in step 1) on to the centre of the cockade.*

Feathers

A feather trim is one of the easiest ways to embellish a hat and can be used to create a variety of looks from the lavish to the simple. Available in their natural shades and in a wide range of dyed colours, feathers can be bought singly and also as mounts, where they are grouped together and fixed on to a base, usually made of net, for more flamboyant trims. Feather trims can also be bought in the form of a hat pin which can be attached to the hat in different positions, depending on the style.

The most opulent feathers are ostrich plumes: rich, flattering and feminine they can be used singly to make a dramatic statement or grouped to soften the edge of a brim. They can be found in almost every hue to complement the fabric of the hat or to add a shock of contrasting colour. For a more understated decoration, natural quill, partridge or pheasant feathers add a jaunty or sporting air to a simple felt hat, and can be purchased from butchers who dress game in the autumn.

To make a Feather trim

This classic feather trim is perfectly matched to the traditional Homburg. The colours tone well, but the iridescent feathers add a touch of gloss to an otherwise plain hat.

1   *Wire groups of fine short feathers together with fuse wire. Add a few longer feathers.*

These three hats show how feathers can be used for quite different effects. The hat at top uses feathers dyed the same colour as the hat to blend but add shape and movement. The green hat features a flamboyant ostrich plume, which provides a strong contrast in colour. The cocktail hat uses two partridge feathers to extend the shape. (*Right: Herald and Heart Hatters*)

2 *Brush the quill ends of the feathers with glue and push into a brooch finding.*

Sparkling trims

Beads of various materials have been used to adorn garments since prehistoric times. In more recent years, beads were used extensively to decorate Victorian and Edwardian costume, and are especially synonymous with the dazzling clothes of the 1920s and 1970s.

Jewellery in the form of brooches or chains made of metal, stones or diamanté, used singly or grouped, make effective hat decorations. Lightweight beads and buttons can be simply glued. Some stones come with mounts which can be pushed through a felt or straw, others come with holes and these may be sewn into position. Sequins are available singly or sewn onto a strip of fine cloth.

As shown in the hats featured here, light-reflecting trims such as these may be used for a stylish, blatant or delicate effect. Cover a hat completely in richly coloured gemstones and the effect will be startling. Alternatively, decorate just a small area of the hat, using sequins or beads to form a motif such as a leaf, heart or name, for a more subtle design.

The variety of beads, sequins and diamanté available to the hat maker is breathtaking. The black hat takes the subtle approach with a few beads, sequins and buttons scattered about to give a hint of decoration. The crown-shaped hat on the right, made from crushed velvet, uses sequin strips to encompass large coloured stones imitating real emeralds and rubies. The hat on the left uses a much more subtle approach with pearls set in between iridescent appliquéd shapes. (*Left: clockwise from top: Ellen Bonner, Bevali Read, Abigail Mill*)

Both of the hats in this picture feature the use of rich fabrics for decoration and embellishment. The hat in the foreground is constructed from resist-dyed velvet which has been heavily embroidered with gold and metallic blue thread. The edges are hand rolled and then decorated with simple bold stitching. The hat in the background is fairly conventional with a small crown and large sweeping brim; it is the rich decoration and use of gold braiding, piping, ribbon and fabric which make this hat stunning. (*Right:* from top: *Herald and Heart Hatters, Judy Clayton.*)

To apply Sequins and beads

Brighten up a plain felt beret with light-reflecting leaf-shaped sequins. Sequins are available in many colours and shapes, so choose designs to suit day or evening wear, or even the season.

1 *Applying individual sequins to a hat can be time consuming, but the effect is well worth the effort. Sew the sequins in place and anchor in position with tiny rocaille beads.*

Band straw

As has been mentioned previously, straw hoods are available ready for blocking, but straw is also manufactured in strips which can be used to make complete hats. Band straw is most commonly used as a trim, however, and it comes in a wide variety of colours, textured patterns and widths. Band straw can be used to neaten the edge of a brim, or as a hatband. Add texture to a straw hat by sewing the trim flat to the crown and/or brim, creating geometric, arabesque or stylized flower designs. Alternatively, for a three-dimensional trim, fold loops of straw in the hand until a pleasing shape is formed, then wire the ends together and stitch to the side or front of a hat. Cover the ends of the trim with a hatband or another trim.

To attach a Straw trim

Revitalize an old straw hat with a new straw trim decorating the crown and brim. Use the trim as a simple band and edging, as here, or cover the brim or crown, or both, with geometric or curved designs to suit the occasion.

1 Remove any existing hatband and trim from the straw. Glue the band straw trim to cover the join between the crown and brim.

*T*his straw hat has been simply decorated with black straw trim forming a zigzag pattern over the brim. Strong colour contrast and the bold geometric design results in a stunning hat. (*Right: Nicola Spillett*)

*S*traw trim can be used to accomplish quite varied effects as shown here. The hat at centre top is edged with a pretty zigzag trim. Orange trim has been used to complement the colour of the straw on the left, and is curled and furled to make an interesting pattern. For the very feminine hat on the right, the trim has been applied to the wide translucent hatband rather than to the straw itself. (*Below:* clockwise from top: *Herald and Heart Hatters, Herald and Heart Hatters, Gil Fox*)

2 *Glue a wider straw trim to the edge of the brim where it is wired or turned over. Straw trim can also be sewn to the hat using stab stitches.*

Veiling, nets & lace

Veiled hats can be extremely flattering, conferring a sense of mystery and allure on the wearer. Extremely popular during the Victorian era and in the 1930s and 1940s, face-concealing veils are still used today on cocktail hats and more widely as a general trim, gathered together to form bows or 'frou-frous', or draped over the crown or around the brim of a dress hat. A veil which covers the face should be shaped on a block so that it stands out from the features slightly.

Veiling is available in many forms: fine, coarse, large or small mesh, plain weave or with chenille spots or glitter. It can be further decorated with beads, ribbons or sequins. For example, for an atmospheric cocktail hat, decorate black veiling with gold or silver sequins in unusual shapes such as moons and stars.

Net can be used in the same way as veiling. The advantage is that net is available in a wider range of colours and woven designs, and yet, like veiling, can be fine and soft or rigid depending on the grade. It does not fray so cut edges can be left unfinished or decorated, if wished, with a trim to complement the hat.

Lace is ideal to use as a soft and feminine hat trimming. It can even be used to cover a foundation shape for a totally lace hat. For lace appliqué, stiffen the material by sewing to a net foundation.

*B*oth straws and felts can be decorated with lace and nets. The straw with the large brim is swathed in a sausage of net. The felt has gold-edged black lace embedded in the upturn between the crown and the brim. (*Left: Herald and Heart Hatters*)

To make a Veil

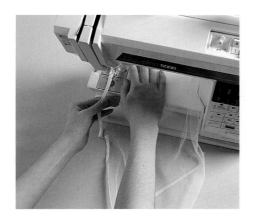

1 Cut the net to twice the length of the finished train. Edge the net on all four sides with satin ribbon, to neaten.

2 Fold the train in half widthways and neatly gather around the fabric circle. Secure with a few stitches.

3 To finish, attach a ready-made white satin bow to the veil where it joins the fabric circle.

The nets on veiled head-dresses can soon become dirty or damaged and need replacing, or you may wish to change the veiling to give a new look to a bridesmaid's circlet. The wedding head-dress used here is made from a circle of satin fabric stuffed with wadding. This is in turn covered with a sausage of net gathered at intervals and decorated with flowers.

Adapting hats

Often a bought hat will have a minimal trim or one of poor quality, but the shape and colour may make the hat worth buying. It is often the prohibitive price of hand work which accounts for poor trimming; this is where your skill and ingenuity come in.

Ideas for Adapting felts

Many of the ideas for adapting straws (see overleaf) may be used for adapting felts. Felts however have the added bonus of being slightly heavier so they can often carry weightier decorations such as diamanté.

- If you have an old felt hat you no longer use, rather than throw it out, cut it up and use it to decorate a contrasting colour felt. Twist or plait felt to make a decorative band or cut out shapes, perhaps leaves or flowers, to appliqué on to another hat.

- Cut a wavy outline around a brim and decorate with a decorative cord, or bind the edge with ribbon.

- Use a hole punch with various size holes to make a decorative border to a brim, or use pinking shears for a zigzag edge.

- Using scissors or a sharp craft knife, cut shapes in the crown of a hat and then line the hat with a contrasting colour so that it shows through.

- Make patterns using metallic studs (like bikers use on their leathers). Studs are available shaped as pyramids, stars, cones or circles and come in silver or gold. They have claws underneath by which to attach them.

- Use velvet to cover the underside of a brim or to make a hatband.

- Appliqué with suede or leather.

- Embroider with wools, silks or embroidery threads.

- Attach homemade or bought tassels or pom-poms.

- Add fringing, frogging or other unusual trims.

- Strap a leather belt with a good buckle around the crown.

From the same basic-shaped felt five different 'looks' have been achieved. The beige felt has been given a wired garland of fruits, leaves and buds. The red felt has a simple criss-cross of red metallic and purple velvet ribbons. The maroon hat features a woven ribbon design. To do this, very carefully mark with tailors' chalk and then cut vertical lines from the brim edge to the brim edge on the other side. Weave ribbon in and out and sew the ends of each piece of ribbon on to the underside of the hat. The black bowler makes use of some very pretty white and metallic woven ribbon. It is tied as a hatband and then one end is cut in a V shape to stop it fraying. The bright blue bowler is wrapped in twisted fabric: a lush silk stretch velvet below with a tighter twist of purple silk above. (*Above*)

Ideas for Adapting berets

A beret is one of the most inexpensive and versatile hats you can buy. Get an original from France or buy them in a variety of colours from department stores. Then let your imagination run riot and decorate; here are a few ideas.

- Punch holes and add eyelets.

- Add a line of cord or frogging with a tassel at the end.

- Sew a brightly coloured woven braid on to the edge to make a hatband.

- Cut two berets in half and then join the different coloured halves together. Cover the join with brightly coloured bias binding.

- Add a velvet or satin ribbon band to the edge and attach a bow with a large diamanté stone in the middle.

- Use an old zip to make a spiral pattern from the centre to the edge.

- Cover in souvenir cloth badges or display a collection of metal badges.

- Use bias binding to make intricate interwoven Celtic patterns.

Clockwise from top left: the black beret is decorated with large diamanté stones for evening wear. The blue beret is decorated with red velvet rouleaux. Work out the desired pattern before you begin and pin the ribbon into place first; remove the pins as you sew. The green beret is covered with tiny ribbon rose-buds. These were glued with a fabric glue, but they can also be sewn in place. The blue beret is covered with plastic silver-backed stars. The brown beret is covered with felt 'paint blobs' and finished with two paintbrushes. The red beret is decorated with green felt holly leaves and berries made from oblong red wooden beads sewn in clusters in the centres of the leaves.

Ideas for Adapting straws

Straws are the hats of summer. They may be very smart and made of expensive fine straws with crisp, clear trims or they may be pretty, summery and dainty with the addition of a fresh flower or ribbon trim.

Holiday straws can be quickly adapted to match your clothes with a simple scarf trim. Just twist or knot a suitable scarf round the hat and tuck under, or tie a reef knot to hold in place.

● Cut away the crown and either machine under the raw edge or pull away strands from the crown and brim to give a feathered edge.

● Straws may be dyed in cold-water fabric dyes, but they will lose their shape and will need to be re-blocked. If you don't want to re-block, colour them with a spray paint which is oil- or acrylic-based.

● Net may be added to make a veil. Look out for brightly dyed nylon net to add to holiday hats.

● Thread stones or shells with holes on to leather thongs or metallic shirring elastic.

● Line the inside of a brim with pretty lace or net.

● Embroider with raffia. Add ears of corn or other natural grasses to the hatband.

Plain straws may be altered to suit your mood and style by the simplest adaptations. Alter the colour with the use of fabric dyes or spray paints; adorn with fabric roses, a scarf or just tie a piece of sea grass or straw round the crown; or embroider a simple flower in tones to suit the colour of the straw. (*Left:* clockwise from top: *Bailey and Tomlin, Viv Knowland, Gil Fox*)

Care of hats

Hats need to be carefully stored in hat boxes to keep their shape. These attractive hat boxes have been decorated with decoupage. To do this at home, buy or collect pictures, cut them out and stick on to a plain or painted box. Apply a coat of varnish to finish.
(*Emma Whitfield*)

Unless the desired look is crumpled, a hat should always look fresh! It is worth investing in a hat box, available from most department stores. Sometimes these are plain but often they come with the company logo.

Line the box with a ring of tissue paper and put the hat inside, crown downwards. If the hat has a large brim, make a cardboard support for the brim to stop it drooping. Flowers should be given a tissue paper surround. Do not rest hats on top of one another.

Remove hairs, fur and bits from felts with the sticky side of a piece of masking tape. Rub a piece of dry bread over a pale or white felt to remove dirty marks. Trimmings are often the first thing to fade, droop or date a hat. Change the trimming and give the hat a new lease of life. Remember, most straws and felts are not designed to be worn in the rain. Felts will shrink and straws will droop! You can dye, re-block, or cut up an old hat; keep the crowns from old straws and felts and use one as a base for a cocktail hat.

PRACTICALITIES

Before embarking on any of the projects described in Creating Hats, take some time to read through this section. It details some professional millinery and standard sewing techniques you may need to practise first. Here, you will also find which materials are available for milliners' and dressmakers' hats; and what specialist equipment will be needed. The standard techniques are used again and again and are quite simple to perfect, especially with the aid of the detailed diagrams that accompany the instructions. Learn how to wire brims, make headbands, and block (shape by steaming, moulding and pressing) felt and straw hats. Also described are the millinery terms for the various components of a hat, and the various sewing and embroidery stitches used throughout the book.

Anatomy of a hat

Before beginning to think about making a hat it is a good idea to know the general terms used to describe the various components of a hat.

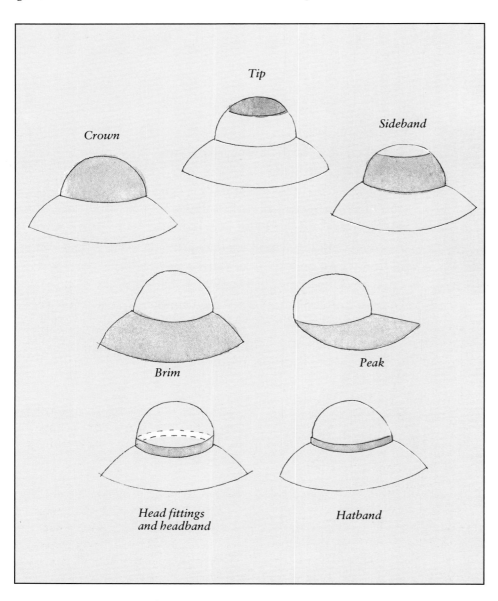

Crown

Tip

Sideband

Brim

Peak

Head fittings and headband

Hatband

Crown
The crown is the part of the hat which sits above the brim. It may be made in one piece or from sections.

Tip
The name given to the uppermost part of the crown. The tip is usually oval in shape.

Sideband
The sideband is the lower part of a one- or two-section crown, beneath the tip and above the brim. It is usually joined at the centre back.

Brim
The brim sits below the crown. It may be large or small and it may be upturned, flat or downturned.

Peak
A peak is the front projecting brim on a cap. It does not go all the way round the cap.

Head fitting and headband
The line inside the crown which touches the head. This is where the headband – a petersham band – is sewn and adjusted so that the hat will fit.

Hatband
The outside band which fits round the outside of the head fitting. This often covers the line where a brim is joined on to a crown.

Tools & equipment

Most of the projects in this book can be made without specialist equipment; however it is useful to know what specialist materials and tools are used in millinery. Also itemized here are some readily available basic items that will prove very useful to the home hat maker.

A collection of wooden crown and brim blocks, hat stands and a fabric dolly head.

Blocks

Skull block

It is not necessary for the amateur hat maker to buy a large variety of blocks, however it is useful to have a skull block to serve as a stand when manipulating or working on a hat. A skull block is made of wood and is head-shaped; it should be the size of the person for whom the hat is being made.

To measure for a skull block: measure round the head from the top of the forehead to just under the bulge at the back of the head for the head size; and from the centre forehead over the head to the centre back for crown depth. These measurements can be marked on the block for the correct fitting.

Block stand

A block stand is used to support the block while working on a hat. One stand will fit a variety of blocks.

Brim block

As the name suggests, this block is used for making brims. It can be either attached to a crown or separate. A

smaller block is more useful than a large one as larger sizes may be taken from it.

Dome block

This is an oval, symmetrical block, used for blocking bowler-shaped crowns.

Linen or dolly head

Made from linen, a dolly head – a linen head – is a lightweight head that is easy to work on.

Ring block

These are wooden rings which may be round or oval in shape. They are used for steaming and stretching trimmings and brims.

Shaped blocks

Wooden blocks can be made in many different shapes for any style of hat according to fashion and popularity. These may be anything: trilby, fez, sailor and many others.

The basics

Pliers

A good pair of pliers is needed for bending and cutting wire. Those with narrow ends are best for turning corners in the wire.

Scissors

At least two pairs will be useful: paper scissors for cutting spartre and other foundation shapes and paper patterns, and dressmaking scissors with a 20 cm (8 in) blade for fabrics.

Brushes

These are needed for lifting the pile of velvets and smoothing long-haired piles of panne and melusine-type fabrics. Some cheap 2.5 cm (1 in) paintbrushes for applying stiffener are also needed.

Craft knife

A sharp craft knife is needed for cutting felts on the block.

Geometry equipment

A ruler, protractor, pencil, and dressmakers' grid paper are required for making paper patterns.

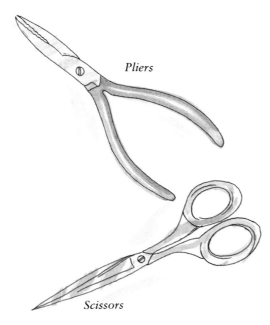

Pliers

Scissors

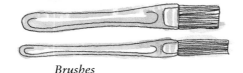

Brushes

Craft knife

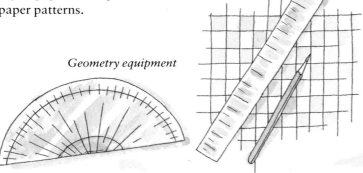

Geometry equipment

Dressmakers' steel pins

Long dressmakers' pins 2.9 cm (1⅛ in) long are used for most work. Lillikin pins, which are very fine, are used for fine silks and expensive velvets. Never steam fabrics with pins in place or they will mark.

Needles

Millinery needles are known as straws. They come in a variety of sizes. As a rule of thumb, the finer the fabric the finer the needle required. The exception to this rule is leather and suede which both need a fine needle. Use sizes 5–6 for heavy block spartre work; 7–8 for felts and foundation shapes; 9–10 for satins, chiffon and very fine work. A heavy, curved needle is useful for blocking.

Thimble

A thimble is essential as a great deal of pressure is needed when pushing needles through heavy block work. A metal one is better than a plastic one.

Tape measure

A non-stretch tape measure is best for accurate measurements.

Tailors' chalk

For transferring designs on to hats; it can be rubbed out quite easily.

Drawing pins

These are used when blocking. They come under considerable strain so they must be strong.

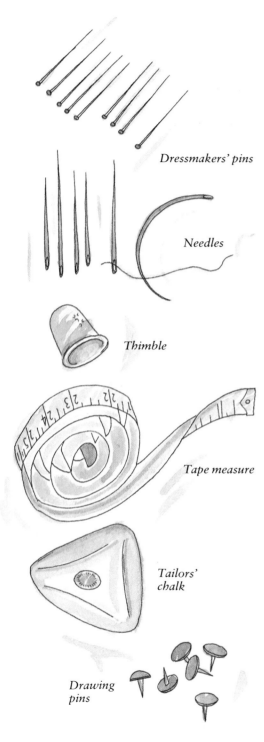

Dressmakers' pins

Needles

Thimble

Tape measure

Tailors' chalk

Drawing pins

Sewing machine

A sewing machine is not used often in millinery, except for making fabric hats, sewing linings and top stitching – however it is essential for many of the projects in this book. A model with a free arm makes the sewing of brims much easier.

Iron

Buy as lightweight an iron as possible, as it will have to be held in the air quite often. A travelling iron is ideal.

Egg iron

This is a special type of iron shaped – as the name suggests – like an egg. It has a long stem on a wooden handle which fits into a clamp fastened on the edge of the table. It is used for shaping felts and draped styles.

Pressing pad

As much of the pressing has to be done in the hand, it is necessary to have a pad on which to hold the work. This can be made by folding a piece of cotton fabric over several times and machining it all over to make a compressed pad about 10 cm (4 in) square.

Kettle

Because materials have to be pulled, eased and stretched into shape, heat and steam are an important part of hat making. Although you can buy large steamers for the purposes of home hat making, a domestic kettle will do very well. The best kind is an old-fashioned type without an automatic switch off.

Sewing machine

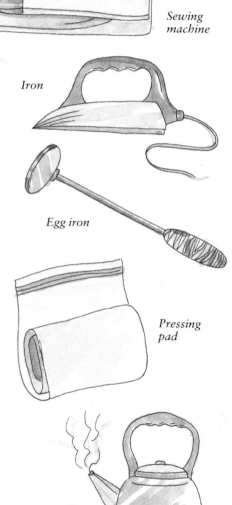

Iron

Egg iron

Pressing pad

Kettle

Materials

This section has been divided into four categories, commencing with pre-manufactured felt and straw hoods ready for blocking into various shapes. The second division details foundation and construction materials; these are the materials used for blocking hats in the same way that a professional milliner would. Thirdly, materials recommended for covering foundation shapes, and lastly, fabrics to use for simple dressmakers' hats.

FELT & STRAW HOODS

Hood is the term used to describe straws and felts as they come pre-manufactured to the milliner ready for blocking. There are two basic shapes: the *cone* is almost fez-like in shape but larger in size and is usually turned into brimless or small-brimmed hats; the *capeline* comes with a brim and is larger than the cone, and is suitable for blocking into larger hats with brims. Both felt and straw hoods are available in a wide variety of colours, qualities and finishes.

Felt has been used for making hats from the time of the ancient Egyptians. Because of its structure it is an excellent material for hat making. A good felt is made of fur and the fibres are not woven but matted together in steam, and therefore can be stretched in every direction. For hand millinery fur felt is preferable to wool felt, which is not so sympathetic to blocking as it tends to shrink and fluff up.

Natural and imitation straws come in such a wide range that it would be impossible to list them all.

Peach bloom
This fur felt has a soft, velvety pile sometimes known as velour. It is obtainable in capeline and cone-shaped hoods. It needs careful handling to avoid marking.

Melusine
This is a high-grade fur felt, sometimes hard to find these days, which is made in a range of beautiful colours. Care is needed when handling these felts but they are tougher than peach bloom.

Mouflon
Similar in appearance to melusine, mouflon is not so silky. Available in pastel shades or two-tone effect, this material is, like melusine, not so easy to find.

Exotic straws
These are usually highly polished such as Baku, parisisal, buntal, Bangkok, Panama, Manila, sisal. They come from Far Eastern countries where traditionally the straw is woven into hoods and then blocked into capeline shapes and polished.

Real Italian straws
This category includes natural straws such as leghorn which is usually made into capeline hoods. Fancy band and pedal straws come into this group. They are not easy to handle but have great charm when made up.

Imitation straws
Examples include cellophane straws from Switzerland and paper from China. They are very popular and are available in hoods and as band straw in various widths.

Pedaline
Similar to pedal straws, this is in fact imitation straw and not as long-lasting as natural straw.

FOUNDATION & CONSTRUCTION MATERIALS

Foundation fabrics are those from which some basic hat shapes are constructed, before being covered in chosen fabrics.

Spartre
This is the most widely used of all foundation shapes. It is a woven straw sheet covered in muslin (cheesecloth) which when dampened can be shaped or blocked and will retain its shape when it dries. It comes in fine and

A collection of materials for making blocked hats including felt and straw hoods, spartre shapes, a dolly stand, millinery wire and stiffener.

heavy versions. It is used for making foundation shapes to be covered with heavier materials such as velvets and satins. It is also used for handmade blocks for both brims and crowns. The muslin-covered side is the right side, and gives a smooth surface under the covering fabric.

Blocking nets
Nets of various kinds are used for shape making when a backing for a lighter fabric is required, such as chiffon, georgette, lace, organza and tulle. Net can be blocked double if extra strength is needed.

Tarlatan
This is a fine net most useful for mounting fabric, which can be used for pattern making. It is also a good interfacing for making unblocked hats.

Stiffened lawn
This is used for unblocked dressmakers' hats.

Domette
A stretchy, woollen fabric, it is used as an interfacing under fine foundation materials to stop any mistakes on the foundation block showing – also known as Mulling.

Millinery wire
This is wire covered in fine cotton thread. It is used for firming up brim edges and making headbands. It comes in various gauges: No 24 is a lace wire and is used for fine work, No 6 is a general-purpose wire, and No 90 is used for making spartre blocks. Ribbon wire is stranded wire woven into tapes and used for making bows and trimmings. Piping wire is a soft, thick, fabric-covered wire.

Stiffeners
Stiffeners are types of varnish used to give body to straw, fabric or felt, and to help them retain a good shape. They are usually applied with a brush to the inside of a hat after the final steaming. The hat should not be handled until the stiffener is dry and no steaming should be done after it has been applied. *Straw varnish* gives a sheen to straw. It may be painted on the right side but only after all the steaming is complete. *Felt stiffener* or Feltene is a special stiffening varnish made for felts. It should be painted on sparingly after all steaming is finished.

Spartalac
This is a thick white liquid brushed evenly on spartre blocks when block making. It forms a hard coating. Spartalac thinners are available to dilute the liquid when it becomes thick and unmanageable.

Rubber solution
This is used for sticking covering materials to difficult foundation shapes, especially on concave parts. It is also used in the making of trimmings and to hold a part of a trimming to a hat.

Sewing threads
Black and white cotton are used for basic work.

Linings
Linings are used to neaten hat crowns if the insides are untidy. Crown linings can be purchased ready-made.

Petersham ribbon
This ribbon is the most common of trimming ribbons. It may also be used for head fitting and for edging brims. It is corded and curves easily.

COVERING MATERIALS FOR USE IN MILLINERY

In theory any material can be used to cover a hat, but in practice there are a few which particularly lend themselves to the craft.

The most important considerations when making blocked hats are whether the fabric can be stretched over a curved surface, steamed and pinned and if, when it is dry, it will retain its blocked shape.

When choosing a fabric remember that it is going to be worn on the head so choose a fabric that is light and comfortable to wear. It is also worth considering if the hat can be cleaned.

Jersey
Lightweight silk and wool jerseys make lovely draped hats. It is not necessary to cut on the bias as jersey is stretchy in all directions.

Lace
For garden party, wedding and cocktail hats, lace is fashionable. Guipure lace may be blocked and stiffened with starch, then mounted on a net foundation, or the motifs can be cut out and made up again on a different net foundation. Large-brimmed picture hats are suited to this material as it can be gathered, draped or left plain.

Laize
This material is sometimes known as straw cloth as it often includes straws in its weave. An ideal fabric for summer hats, it is lightweight and can be used for covering shapes, cut to a pattern and made into interlining. Care must be taken when handling laize as it frays easily.

Leather
Leather and suede to be used for hat making should be very soft and similar in quality to glove leather.

Panne
Long-haired smooth velvet is much used in millinery. The pile can be stroked in any direction.

Satin
A good silk with a dull sheen that will stand crisply in folds is the best type to choose. Shiny satins are not good for hat making as they mark easily and show every crease and irregularity in the shape.

Taffeta
Cheaper taffetas are used for linings. The better-quality ones are used mainly for draped and turban shapes.

Transparent fabrics
The most common ones are chiffon, organza and tulle. They should all be good quality. Real silk gives the best results.

Tulle
Silk tulle is best as it is crisp and will stay in place, whether blocked or draped. Tulle made from nylon is springy and will not hold blocking.

Velvet
Silk pile, cotton-backed velvet is the best choice. Cotton velvets are good and economical for day wear.

FABRICS FOR DRESSMAKERS' HATS

Soft hats can be made from almost any fabric as long as it is not too heavy or too stiff. The same basic pattern can produce a variety of looks just by using different fabrics.

Suitable fabrics for dressmakers' hats include cottons (calico, gingham, seersucker, Liberty Tana lawn, drill, denim and canvas), wools (fine, textured, knitted, woven, tweeds and tartans), corduroy, lace and jersey.

A collection of fabrics for making and decorating milliners' and dressmakers' hats including cottons, silks, organdie, canvas, woollen weaves, lace, leather and suede as well as richer fabrics such as velvets and satins.

Practical techniques

This section describes the techniques involved in making a milliners' hat: blocking felt and straw hoods, wiring brims for a turned or bound edge, and finishing. Also included is how to make a wired headband, which can be used as the basis for a bridal head-dress or combined with spartre crowns. Finally, sewing and decorative embroidery stitches are itemized and illustrated.

Blocking felts

Blocking is the term used to describe the most common method of shaping hats. Methods of working vary considerably in the millinery trade and the great variety in the price of hats is reflected, as in the fashion business, in the way in which a hat is made and the materials used. Inexpensive hats available in department stores are usually produced to a standard size on hydraulically operated metal blocks. At the other end of the spectrum are what are known as model hats. These are blocked by hand on wooden blocks and are individually made to fit a particular client.

As described earlier, blocks come in all shapes and sizes. They are expensive to buy and are not easily found second hand. However a block will help to give you a more professional finish.

In order to block a hat you need a shape to work with. Felt is a particularly good material for blocking. Made from loose fibres which are matted together under pressure and steam, there is no straight grain and consequently when felt is warm and damp it can be stretched in any direction, and when dry will hold its shape well. The best millinery felts are made from fur, usually rabbit. They hold their texture well and can be re-blocked successfully. The quality of wool felt depends on the quality of the sheep's wool from which it is made. Oversteaming causes wool to shrink.

Remember to select the hood according to the style of hat. Choose a cone for making a small brimless hat and a capeline to make a large-brimmed hat. Try to handle the hood as little as possible and do not use too many pins. As a beginner choose dark rather than light colours which will easily show up marks.

Although in the materials section it states that stiffener should be painted on to the inside of your felt after the hat is finished, some milliners prefer to do this before they begin to make their hats (see step 2). It makes the hat harder to handle while blocking but it does eliminate shrinkage.

*A*lways use a capeline hood to make a wide-brimmed hat.

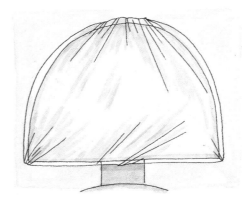

1 Prepare the block by covering it with cling film (plastic wrap) or a dry-cleaning bag. This will prevent a residue of dye staining the block and discolouring the next hat.

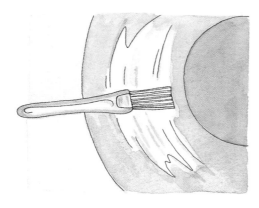

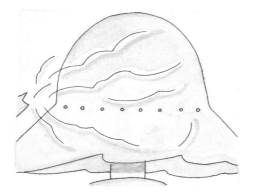

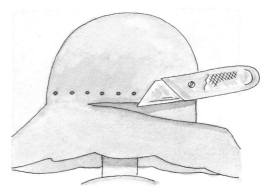

2 If the felt is thin or if it needs a great deal of stretching a little felt stiffener needs to be painted on to the wrong side of the hood. To do this turn the hood inside out, place a pin to mark the starting point and paint the stiffener all over the surface. Let the stiffener dry thoroughly; stains can appear if stiffener and water are mixed together.

3 Hold the hood over the steamer for three to five minutes and let the hot moisture penetrate the felt. Stretch the warm felt over the block. It can then be held in place with either drawing pins or a length of cord just below the head line so that no pin holes will be visible in the finished crown. The position of the head line will depend on whether it is a shallow or deep-crowned hat.

4 Cut away the surplus felt at the head line, starting with a knife and continuing with scissors. Do not cut into the felt which will be used to make the brim.

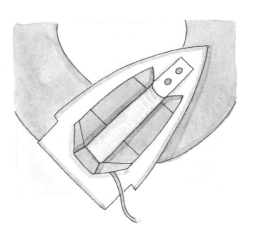

5 The brim is blocked in almost the same way as the crown. The head line needs to be the same measurement as for the crown. The felt can be stretched and shrunk to fit the brim block. Depending on the shape of the brim, steam, stretch and pull the brim over the block and then pin it into position. Pull the work evenly, stretching it first on one side and then on the other to prevent any lumps and bumps forming. Keep steaming and stretching while working using a damp cloth and an iron or a kettle.

Tips

- Brims can be shaped by hand. This requires a great deal of patience and a good eye. Brims can also be pre-shaped on a block and then shaped to a special design with a steamer.

- If the head fitting on a felt brim is too large for the crown after blocking, cut away the extra at the centre back and join with an invisible edge, using grafting stitch.

- If the head fitting on a felt crown is too large for the brim, it can be shrunk using an egg iron.

- After blocking and making, most felts will benefit from a light steaming and a brush to raise the pile.

Blocking straws

The way in which a straw is treated depends on the type of straw being used, as some will stretch more easily than others. But, in common with felts, all straws are treated with a mixture of steam, heat and pressure to force them into shape on a block.

● The simplest way to make a straw hat is to block the crown and brim in one piece.

● Paint the stiffener on to the outside of the straw before putting it on the block. This will give a sheen to the straw and assist with the blocking process.

● Once the stiffener has dried, dampen the straw to soften it. Smooth straws can be very unyielding and need dampening well.

● Pull the straw over the crown block making sure that it is central before pinning. Because straws are woven from the centre of the tip to the base they need to be centred carefully to ensure concentric circles appearing. Synthetic straws may stretch a good deal and will need to be heavily pinned to ensure a smooth finish, particularly over the brim block.

● If blocking the crown and brim separately, do not separate the two parts until the crown has been blocked. Also, make sure that the head measurements, the head lines, are approximately the same for each piece. Block the brim as described for the felt.

Wiring brims

Wire is nearly always used to support the brim edge of a hat. For general work, use gauge 6. As wire comes in a fairly tightly bound roll it must first be straightened otherwise the excess spring in the wire makes it quite unmanageable. To do this, cut the wire with wire cutters and run it back and forth round a chair leg. For wire which has to make a sharp turn rather than a gentle curve, deftly bend it with pliers. *Never* try to break wire by twisting it; cut it with pliers or wire cutters.

The techniques described here for wiring brims for a turned and bound edge are applicable to both felts and straws.

FOR A BOUND EDGE

1 Using wire stitch, sew the wire all round the brim. Stitch the two overlapping wires firmly together when finishing off. The edge can then be bound with petersham ribbon.

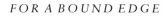

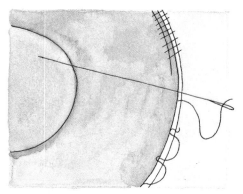

Note: *Measure the wire to the circumference of the brim plus a 5–6 cm (2–2¼ in) overlap. Always start wiring at the back of the brim.*

FOR A TURNED EDGE

1 Using wire stitch, sew the wire to the underside of the brim, 1 cm (³/₈ in) in from the edge. Stitch the two wires together firmly at the overlap. Turn the brim edge over the wire and press.

2 Machine stitch the edge enclosing the wire. Either cut the raw edge along the machine line or turn it in again and slip stitch by hand.

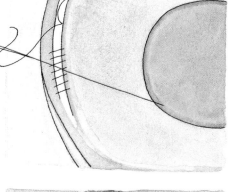

Finishing

Whether you have blocked a straw or a felt hat the following steps complete the process.

1 If the crown and brim have been blocked separately, attach the crown to the brim, matching the centre backs. Pin in position, with the crown over the brim, and sew together using large back stitches.

2 Insert a petersham ribbon over the head fitting, inside the hat, and sew from the inside with stab stitches.

Wired headbands

A wired headband is used for rather specialist purposes by professional milliners. It will be most useful to the amateur hat maker as a basic headband shape, which can be covered with fabric and trimmed for a bridesmaid's or 1920s flapper-style head-dress. It can also be used with pre-formed buckram or spartre shapes, available from department stores. The shape is attached inside the headband, which must be made 1.5 cm (½ in) larger than the head fitting measurement.

1 Cut a 3 × 65 cm (1¼ × 25½ in) bias strip of spartre, buckram or stiff millinery canvas. Join the two ends of the strip together to the required length. Sew wire along the two edges of the headband using wire stitch, overlapping the ends by about 5 cm (2 in). Stitch firmly over both ends.

2 Cut two lengths of tarlatan 5 cm (2 in) wide on the bias and stretch them. Bind the edges of the wire with the tarlatan, by stretching it over the wired edge and attaching with stab stitch. The oval shape of the headband can be made by stretching it over a block of the correct dimensions.

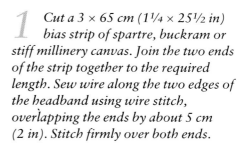

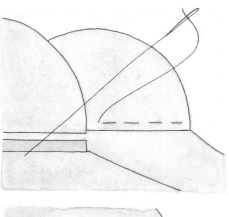

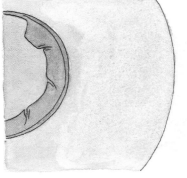

*T*rim with a simple hatband to cover the join between crown and brim.

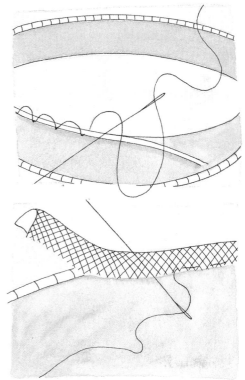

Sewing stitches

There are not many specialist stitches used in millinery; most are the same as those used in dressmaking and needlework. Darning, oversewing and grafting stitches are only used when working with felts.

Darning stitch

This is used for making an invisible edge join, when both sides of the work will show, for example on an upturned brim. Place the felt pieces edge to edge and stitch diagonally through the thickness about 3 mm (⅛ in) either side of the seam. Return the stitch vertically and repeat. The stitches will be opposite each other along the length of the seam.

Wire stitch

This is an extremely important stitch as it is used for holding wire to the edge of brims and headbands. It is like buttonhole stitch with the stitches 1–2 cm (½–¾ in) apart. To start, oversew the wire two or three times to the edge of the brim foundation shape. Make a stitch about 13–19 mm (½–¾ in) from the beginning but behind the wire and push the needle through the brim just underneath the wire. Do not pull tightly. Pull the needle through the back of the loop, pull tightly and repeat. If you put the needle through the front loop rather than the back, it can slip and will not hold the wire firmly. The knot should lie easily on the extreme outside edge of the wire.

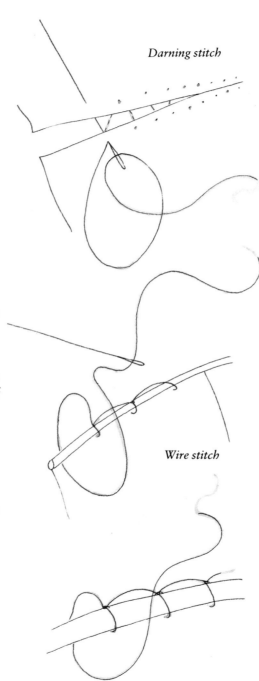

Darning stitch

Wire stitch

Slip stitch

This is the same stitch as used in dressmaking. In millinery it is often used for finishing covered brim edges and inserting linings. To attach folded fabric to a single layer of fabric pass the needle along the inside of the fold and out again, then pick up a small stitch on the flat fabric marginally below the line of the fold and repeat.

Back stitch

This stitch is normally used for joining spartre or joining crowns to brims when the line of stitching is to be covered. Start with a small stitch under the fabric, bringing the thread through and taking it back to the beginning of the stitch. Push through and then bring it out in front of the first stitch. Take it back to the end of that stitch and repeat.

Stab stitch

Stab stitch is used for headbands, attaching trimmings, joining brims to crowns, holding folds in place and block making. The length of stitch will depend on the task. It is made by stabbing the needle neatly and evenly from the inside of the hat to the outside. The long side of the stitch is on the inside of the hat, the outside stitch should barely be visible. If there are many long inside stitches it may be best to cover them with a lining.

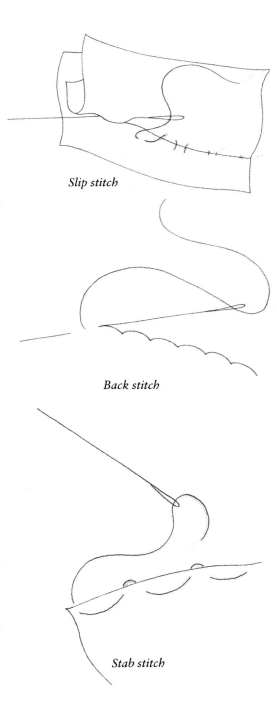

Slip stitch

Back stitch

Stab stitch

Oversewing stitch

This is used for sewing felt together from the wrong side or inside of the join and makes the join extremely strong. It is pressed flat when finished. Place the right sides of the felt together and make a neat, evenly spaced row of stitching along the whole length of the seam, taking the thread through and over the edges of the felt.

Grafting stitch

Grafting stitch is almost the same as oversewing stitch, except that instead of placing the felt with right sides facing it is placed edge to edge. Starting with a small, neat back stitch, work from the wrong side passing the thread through the thickness of the felt so that no stitches show on the right side, but oversewn stitches show on the wrong side. Finish with a back stitch.

Millinery knot

This knot is needed in millinery so that the ends of the thread can be cut off without the need for several back stitches, adding bulk to the hat. First make a knot at the end of the thread by twisting it round the first finger, then rolling the twist into a knot between the thumb and first finger. Hold the knot between the thumb and first finger and wind the thread round the first finger several times, slip the threaded needle behind these threads from the top and, still holding the knot and threads, pull the needle through to make a second knot about 5–8 cm (2–3 in) from the first.

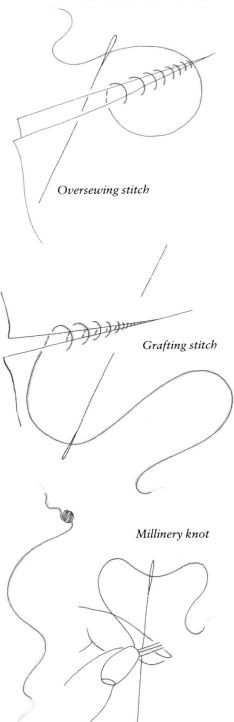

Oversewing stitch

Grafting stitch

Millinery knot

E m b r o i d e r y
s t i t c h e s

Embroidery is often used in millinery to add colour and decoration to a hat, serving to enrich, embellish and emphasize.

The thread should never be so thick as to distort the background fabric or so fine that it is invisible to the eye. The needle must have an eye large enough to hold the thread, but small enough to pass easily through the material without pulling it. The hat to be embroidered must be firm enough to hold the stitches.

Chain stitch
Chain stitch may be used as a border or outline stitch or worked in close rows as a filling stitch. Starting at the top of the line to be stitched, bring the needle through from the back of the fabric at point A. Insert the needle right next to A; bring it out at B. The distance depends on the length of stitch desired. Draw the needle through the fabric and over the loop of working thread.

Stem stitch
Stem stitch can be used for both backgrounds and outlines. Bring the needle through from the back of the fabric. Hold the working thread either to the right or to the left of the needle, but keep the thread consistently on one side. Re-insert the needle at A, bring out at B, and draw the thread through to complete the second stitch.

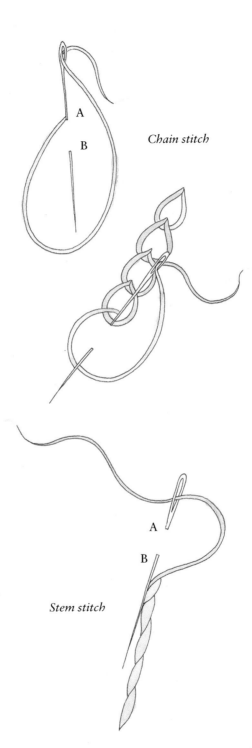

Chain stitch

Stem stitch

Satin stitch
This is a major embroidery stitch and, although it appears simple, it is difficult to get the stitches to lie evenly and close together to give a neat edge. It may be used for filling, geometric patterns and shaded effects. It can be worked in various lengths but very long stitches may become untidy. The stitches may be slanted or lie parallel across the work. To begin, lightly outline the shape with tailors' chalk or a pencil. Start in the centre of the shape and bring the needle through from the back at point A. To establish an angle (if you want a slant) insert the needle at B and bring it out close to A. Work up to the top, then start again at the centre, and work down to the bottom. It is important to maintain a crisp edge by working the stitches evenly next to one another.

Fishbone stitch
This has similarities to satin stitch, but the sloping stitches are worked alternately on the right and the left side under the base of the previous stitch.

Feather stitch
This delicate stitch is also known as coral stitch. It may be used as a filling or as an outline stitch. It is an open-loop stitch made alternately to the left and to the right.

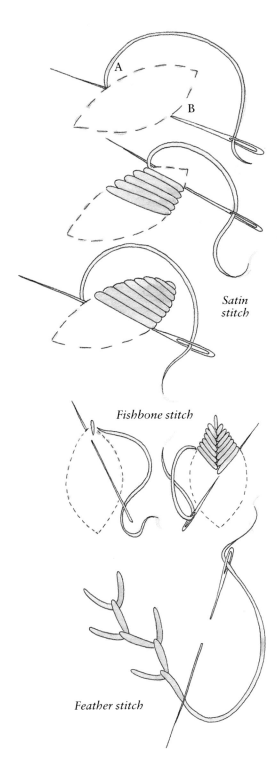

Satin stitch

Fishbone stitch

Feather stitch

Blanket and buttonhole stitch

This stitch is known as buttonhole stitch when the stitches are worked close together. As the name implies, this stitch is used to neaten buttonholes. When the stitches are further apart, this is known as blanket stitch. Blanket stitch is used for decorating hat brims. Work from left to right. Bring the needle through from the back of the fabric at A. Insert the needle at B, bring it out at C, straight down from B and in line with A. Hold the working thread under the needle as shown, to form a straight line along the bottom.

Overcast stitch

When making an appliqué hat, overcast stitch is one way of attaching motifs to the background fabric. It is a small stitch worked at a right angle to the fabric. Pass the needle from the back of the fabric and into the edge of the appliqué shape, making small straight stitches.

French knots

These may be scattered at random over an area to give a textural effect, or they can be placed close together as filling stitches. Bring the needle through from the back of the fabric at point A. Hold the working thread in the left hand and wrap it round the needle once, or twice for a larger knot. Insert the needle right next to A and pull the twists gently until they are snug but not tight round the needle. Then draw the needle through to the back of the work.

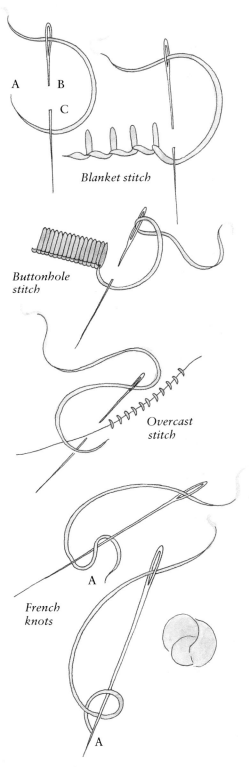

Blanket stitch

Buttonhole stitch

Overcast stitch

French knots

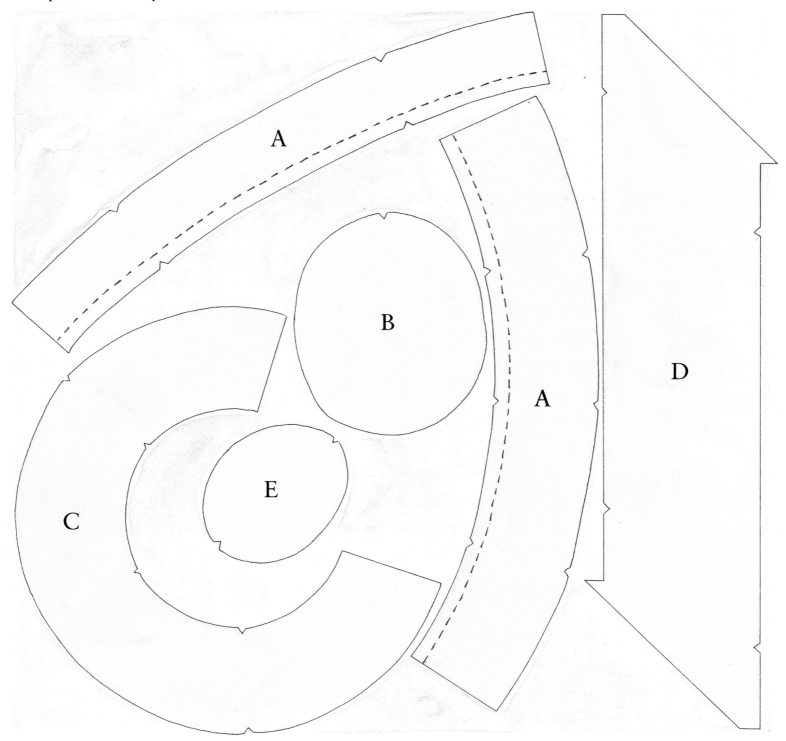

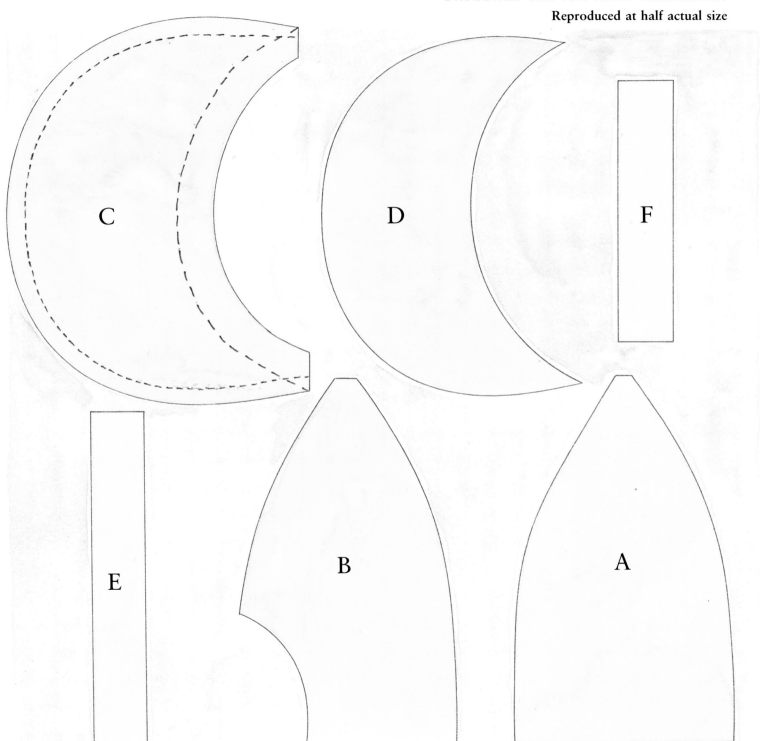

Bibliography

Anlezark, Mildred, *Hats on Heads: The Art of Creative Millinery* (Kangaroo Press, Sydney, 1991).

du Cann, Charlotte, *Vogue Modern Style and How to Achieve It* (Century, London, 1988).

Clark, Fiona, *Hats* (The Costume Accessories Series, BT Batsford Ltd, London, 1982).

Couldridge, Alan, *The Hat Book* (Ventura Publications, London, 1980).

Ginsburg, Madeleine, *The Hat: Trends and Traditions* (Studio Editions, London, 1990).

Morgan, Peter, *Making Hats* (BT Batsford Ltd, London, 1971).

Southern, Anne, *Millinery* (An Arco Publication, USA, 1962).

Thaarup, Aage and Shackell, Dora, *How to Make a Hat* (Cassell and Company, London, 1957).

Contributors

Jennie Atkinson, 10F Hedgegate Court, Powis Terrace, London W11 1JP. Tel: 071 229 2970.

Bailey and Tomlin, Clockwork Studios, 38 Southwell Road, London SE5 4NP. Tel: 071 274 4116.

Lucy Barlow Hats, 14 Portabello Green, London W10 5TZ. Tel: 081 968 5333.

Ellen Bonner, Flat 5, 37 Holmewood Gardens, London SW2 3NA. Tel: 081 671 0378.

Victoria Brown. Tel: 071 708 5559.

Anne Marie Cadman, Textile Designer, 16 Hey Road, Rastrick, Brighouse, Yorks HD6 3LP. Tel: 0484 711757.

Judy Clayton, 64 Queens Road, Farnborough, Hampshire GU14 6DX.

Gilly Forge, 14 Addison Avenue, London W11. Tel: 071 603 3833.

Gil Fox, Worcester. Tel: 0905 29977.

Fred Bare, 118 Columbia Road, London E2 74G. Tel: 071 739 4612.

Katherine Goodison. Tel: 071 828 6498.

Herald and Heart Hatters, 131 St Philip Street, London SW8 3SS. Tel: 071 627 2414.

Herbert Johnson, 30 New Bond Street, London W1Y 9HD. Tel: 071 408 1174.

Mayling Hung, 10 Uppingham Avenue, Stanmore, Middx HA7 2JY. Tel: 081 907 3542.

Sarah King, Waterside, 99 Rotherhithe Street, London SE16 4NF. Tel: 071 237 0017.

Viv Knowland, 6/8 Sedley Place, London W1R 1HQ. Tel: 071 629 2302.

Abigail Mill, 132 Hall Road, Norwich, Norfolk NR1 2PU. Tel: 0603 765032.

Linda Miller, Abbotts Barton Farmhouse, Abbotts Barton, Winchester, Hamps SO23 7HY. Tel: 0962 870789.

Sharon Mitchell, Flat 5, 60 Kelross Road, Highbury, London N5 2QJ. Tel: 071 704 6667.

Monsoon Fashions Ltd, 74 Winslow Road, London W6 9SF.

Bevali Read Hats, 13 Middleton Road, Dalston, London E8 4BL. Tel: 071 254 5760.

Teresa Searle, 43 Monmouth Road, Bishopston, Bristol, Avon BS7 8LG. Tel: 0272 247836.

Nicola Spillett, Flat 2, 76 Ellison Road, Streatham, London. Tel: 081 764 9190.

Tait and Style, Cockpit Workshops, Cockpit Yard, Northington Street, London WC1N 2NP. Tel: 071 831 6212.

Karen Triffitt. Tel: 071 978 2897/0532 886276.

Wendy Watt, Stroud, Gloucs. Tel: 0453 884860.

Emma Whitfield. Tel: 081 674 5220.

Tamsin Young, Studio Ten, Muspole Workshops, 25–27 Muspole Street, Norwich, Norfolk NR3 1DJ. Tel: 0603 760955/0603 624597.

Suppliers

Alma (London) Ltd. Suppliers of leather and suede. Unit D, 12–14 Greatorex Street, London E1 5NF. Tel: 071 375 0343.

Boon and Lane Ltd. Suppliers of blocks, steamers and hat stretchers. 7–11 Taylor Street, Luton, Beds. Tel: 0582 23226.

Borovick Fabrics Ltd. Suppliers of fashion fabrics. 16 Berwick Street, London W1V 4HP. Tel: 071 437 2180.

S.A. Brown Pty Ltd. Millinery suppliers. 2/52 Shepherd Street, Chippendale 2008, Australia.

Janet Coles Beads. Suppliers of hat pins and beads. Perdiwell Cottage, Bilford Road, Worcester WR3 8QA. Tel: 0905 54024.

Paul Craig Ltd. Millinery suppliers. Unit 3, Wealden Business Park, Farningham Road, Crowborough, E Sussex TN6 2JR.

Cunningham & Co (Hatters) Ltd. Millinery suppliers and hat makers. 15 North Street, Andrew Street, Edinburgh EH2 1HJ. Tel: 031 556 5142.

Ells and Farrier Ltd. Suppliers of diamante and sequins. 5 Princes Street, Hanover Square, London W1; Mail order: Unit 26 Chiltern Trading Estate, Earl Howe Road, Holmer Green, High Wycombe, Bucks. Tel: 0494 715606.

Eurostudio. Suppliers of stencil crayons and stencils. Tel: 0582 766331.

MacCulloch and Wallis Ltd. Suppliers of foundation wire and needles. 25–26 Dering Street, London W1 0BH. Tel: 071 629 0311.

The Novelty Import Co. Ltd. Suppliers of feather and flower trims. Michelle House (2nd floor), 45/46 Berners Street, London W1P 3AD. Tel: 071 323 3205.

C M Offray & Son Ltd. Suppliers of ribbons. Fir Tree Place, Church Road, Ashford, Middlesex TW15 2PH.

Pebeo. Suppliers of fabric paints. Art Graphic, Unit 2, Poulton Close, Dover, Kent CT17 0HL. Tel: 0304 242244.

Penny Pins. Suppliers of hat pins. 17 Aynhoe Road, London W14 0QA. Tel: 071 602 7017.

Cyril J Preston Pty Ltd. Millinery suppliers. 258 Flinders Lane, Melbourne 3000, Australia.

Seigle and Stockman Ltd. Suppliers of blocks, dummies, egg irons and stands. 2 Old Street, London EC1V 9AA.

Williams and Delaney. Millinery suppliers and hat makers. Unit 006, The Chandlery, 50 Westminster Bridge Road, London SE1 7QY. Tel: 071 721 7622.

Acknowledgements

I would like to thank all the people who helped to create this book: Jan and Brian for their wonderful photography, and Viv for making real coffee and looking after everyone so well; Cathy for her brilliant styling and optimism; Cecilie Halvorsen, Jack Moxley and Ine Murphy for hand modelling; Felicia Sanabria, Inez Murphy, Zoe Wilkinson, Jessica Moxley, Steven Bawden and Diana, Sophie, and Oliver Hallstrom for modelling hats; all those who made projects for the book and who were happy to give away their trade secrets and all who loaned hats for photography (see Contributors); Dawn from the London College of Fashion who taught me some basic millinery and Lindsay Rosehead, course director at Harrow College, for allowing me to use her students work; Meryl Lloyd for making the fabric roses and Jan Bridge for decorating the babies hats and berets; my family who put up with my eating, sleeping, talking, making and wearing hats for the last year; and Joanna Lorenz, Judith Simons and Cortina Butler for producing the book.

Many thanks also to the following for supplying or loaning materials and props for the book (see Suppliers and Contributors for addresses):

C M Offray & Son Ltd (ribbons); Penny Pins (hat pins); Janet Coles Beads (hat pins and beads); Ells and Farrier Ltd (diamante and sequins); Pebeo (fabric paints); Eurostudio (stencil crayons and stencils); Kangol (berets); Fred Bare (felt hats); Williams and Delaney (props); Herald and Heart Hatters (beads, feathers and trims).

Index